This book belongs to:

____

Aries Daily Horoscope 2024

Mystic Cat
Suite 41906, 3/2237 Gold Coast HWY
Mermaid Beach, Queensland, 4218
Australia
islandauthor@hotmail.com

The information accessible from this book is for informational purposes only. No statement within is a promise of benefits. There is no guarantee of any results.

Images are under license from Shutterstock, Dreamstime, Canva, or Depositphotos.

Contents

2024

January

S	M	T	W	T	F	S
	1	2	3	4	5	6
7	8	9	10	11	12	13
14	15	16	17	18	19	20
21	22	23	24	25	26	27
28	29	30	31			

February

S	M	T	W	T	F	S
				1	2	3
4	5	6	7	8	9	10
11	12	13	14	15	16	17
18	19	20	21	22	23	24
25	26	27	28	29		

March

S	M	T	W	T	F	S
					1	2
3	4	5	6	7	8	9
10	11	12	13	14	15	16
17	18	19	20	21	22	23
24	25	26	27	28	29	30
31						

April

S	M	T	W	T	F	S
	1	2	3	4	5	6
7	8	9	10	11	12	13
14	15	16	17	18	19	20
21	22	23	24	25	26	27
28	29	30				

May

S	M	T	W	T	F	S
			1	2	3	4
5	6	7	8	9	10	11
12	13	14	15	16	17	18
19	20	21	22	23	24	25
26	27	28	29	30	31	

June

S	M	T	W	T	F	S
						1
2	3	4	5	6	7	8
9	10	11	12	13	14	15
16	17	18	19	20	21	22
23	24	25	26	27	28	29
30						

July

S	M	T	W	T	F	S
	1	2	3	4	5	6
7	8	9	10	11	12	13
14	15	16	17	18	19	20
21	22	23	24	25	26	27
28	29	30	31			

August

S	M	T	W	T	F	S
				1	2	3
4	5	6	7	8	9	10
11	12	13	14	15	16	17
18	19	20	21	22	23	24
25	26	27	28	29	30	31

September

S	M	T	W	T	F	S
1	2	3	4	5	6	7
8	9	10	11	12	13	14
15	16	17	18	19	20	21
22	23	24	25	26	27	28
29	30					

October

S	M	T	W	T	F	S
		1	2	3	4	5
6	7	8	9	10	11	12
13	14	15	16	17	18	19
20	21	22	23	24	25	26
27	28	29	30	31		

November

S	M	T	W	T	F	S
					1	2
3	4	5	6	7	8	9
10	11	12	13	14	15	16
17	18	19	20	21	22	23
24	25	26	27	28	29	30

December

S	M	T	W	T	F	S
1	2	3	4	5	6	7
8	9	10	11	12	13	14
15	16	17	18	19	20	21
22	23	24	25	26	27	28
29	30	31				

2025

January

S	M	T	W	T	F	S
			1	2	3	4
5	6	7	8	9	10	11
12	13	14	15	16	17	18
19	20	21	22	23	24	25
26	27	28	29	30	31	

February

S	M	T	W	T	F	S
						1
2	3	4	5	6	7	8
9	10	11	12	13	14	15
16	17	18	19	20	21	22
23	24	25	26	27	28	

March

S	M	T	W	T	F	S
						1
2	3	4	5	6	7	8
9	10	11	12	13	14	15
16	17	18	19	20	21	22
23	24	25	26	27	28	29
30	31					

April

S	M	T	W	T	F	S
		1	2	3	4	5
6	7	8	9	10	11	12
13	14	15	16	17	18	19
20	21	22	23	24	25	26
27	28	29	30			

May

S	M	T	W	T	F	S
				1	2	3
4	5	6	7	8	9	10
11	12	13	14	15	16	17
18	19	20	21	22	23	24
25	26	27	28	29	30	31

June

S	M	T	W	T	F	S
1	2	3	4	5	6	7
8	9	10	11	12	13	14
15	16	17	18	19	20	21
22	23	24	25	26	27	28
29	30					

July

S	M	T	W	T	F	S
		1	2	3	4	5
6	7	8	9	10	11	12
13	14	15	16	17	18	19
20	21	22	23	24	25	26
27	28	29	30	31		

August

S	M	T	W	T	F	S
					1	2
3	4	5	6	7	8	9
10	11	12	13	14	15	16
17	18	19	20	21	22	23
24	25	26	27	28	29	30
31						

September

S	M	T	W	T	F	S
	1	2	3	4	5	6
7	8	9	10	11	12	13
14	15	16	17	18	19	20
21	22	23	24	25	26	27
28	29	30				

October

S	M	T	W	T	F	S
			1	2	3	4
5	6	7	8	9	10	11
12	13	14	15	16	17	18
19	20	21	22	23	24	25
26	27	28	29	30	31	

November

S	M	T	W	T	F	S
						1
2	3	4	5	6	7	8
9	10	11	12	13	14	15
16	17	18	19	20	21	22
23	24	25	26	27	28	29
30						

December

S	M	T	W	T	F	S
	1	2	3	4	5	6
7	8	9	10	11	12	13
14	15	16	17	18	19	20
21	22	23	24	25	26	27
28	29	30	31			

2024

Daily Horoscope

"Astrology is a Language. If you understand this language, The Sky Speaks to You."
—Dane Rudhyar

<u>January</u>

Sun	Mon	Tue	Wed	Thu	Fri	Sat
	1	2	3	4 	5	6
7	8	9	10	11 	12	13
14	15	16	17	18 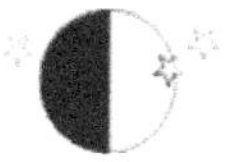	19	20
21	22	23	24	25 	26	27
28	29	30	31			

NEW MOON

Wolf Moon

JANUARY

1 Monday

A communitive element in the air brings news as people reach out to sync up with you. It offers social engagement and a lively atmosphere that underscores the undercurrents of change that sweep in to help you chase dreams and nurture your life. It provides social options that allow you to gain traction in developing life by sharing thoughts and ideas with others who grow your world. Lovely changes ahead bring happiness and connection.

2 Tuesday

The planet Mercury turns direct, and this positive cosmic change highlights expansion around your social life. It clears the way forward and lets you harness a sense of wanderlust as you engage in an active and lively time. It brings a purposeful path towards sharing with others who draw well-being into your life. As you notice the rhythm and pace picking up speed, you discover room to improve your social life.

3 Wednesday

Setting your sights on expanding your life brings positive change that harnesses the essence of adventure. As you raise the barriers and embark on a journey of discovery, the winds of change carry you forward towards developing unique areas that speak to your soul. It helps you kick off a journey of rising prospects with the added benefit of improving your circumstances.

4 Thursday

The planet Mars sets up camp in Capricorn, and this planetary alignment creates a stable foundation to develop your working goals. Increasing drive attracts an ambitious focus to help you meet the challenges as you build your career path. Capricorn lends more security to the process of developing your goals. It enables you to create tangible progress by developing a stable blueprint for future growth. It brings an expressive chapter that builds sound foundations in your world.

5 Friday

As the path ahead clears, you gain a deeper understanding of where you seek to head in your life. It brings opportunities to mingle, connecting you with thoughtful and supportive friends and companions. The happy news on the winds of change brings fresh energy into your life. It offers a positive aspect that is a cause for celebration as you get busy expanding the horizons in your social life.

6 Saturday

Beautiful changes ahead shift your focus towards developing your social circle. It offers progress and potential that promotes a compelling journey of enriching time shared with others. You attract a profound sense of connection that nurtures well-being and harmony. As your schedule fills up with new opportunities, it gives you a chance to grow meaningful bonds and entertain with friends. It cracks the code to extend life outwardly.

7 Sunday

A serendipitous snippet of news brings a stroke of luck. It opens a journey that inspires change as it leads to an unexpected breakthrough in your social life. A situation you invest time and energy into developing blossoms. It offers companionship and brings a time for engaging in lively discussions as your circle of friends expands. It adds a dash of creativity and excitement to your life.

8 Monday

Life picks up steam as events ahead set in motion exciting possibilities. It opens a journey that draws happiness and harmony. You get involved with a venture that supports your dreams. Things are on the move, and moving beyond your comfort zone offers remarkable growth. Chasing success drives your vision forward towards an upward trend that offers rising prospects. Being proactive lets, you take action and gain a foothold in achieving your dreams.

9 Tuesday

Mercury Square Neptune brings new insight into your life. Imagination rises, providing unique ideas and heightened problem-solving abilities. Life lightens by degrees as you step out on a new journey forward in your life. Notable changes help you hone in on new possibilities that offer growth and rising prospects. A unique area calls your name and takes you towards developing projects and endeavors that see you working with your creativity.

10 Wednesday

The Mars sextile Saturn aspect brings drive and energy to your daily tasks. Your powers of endurance heighten, enabling you to deal with all the activities on your plate and still have excess energy to burn. It jumpstarts a time of rising prospects and prosperity that help you head towards growth. A significant energy buildup offers improvement by providing innovative solutions that sweeten your life on many levels.

11 Thursday

Today, a New Moon offers the chance to plan goals and create the blueprint for future growth. You soon hit your stride in a lively environment that provides a lovely rhythm and pace. It promotes movement and discovery, enabling you to access rising possibilities worth your time. Indeed, plenty of new happenings and invitations keep you optimistic about prospects. You discover a new joy in life, promoting a bustling and productive environment.

12 Friday

The Mars trine Jupiter aspect brings a boost to your spirits. It offers a favorable influence that puts the wind back in your sails. Life brings lovely changes as something inspirational comes your way that nurtures happiness in your world. It helps you find your groove in a grounded environment that lets you focus on areas that bring peace and harmony. It enables you to sail towards smoother waters on a journey filled with promise.

13 Saturday

Life picks up steam as a group environment triggers options that encourage collaboration. It brings invitations that draw lively energy into your social life. A change of scenery renews motivation and promotes lively discussions and the development of unique goals and projects which catch your interest. Socialising and networking bring opportunities to share with like-minded people who boost morale.

14 Sunday

Mercury enters your 10th house of ambitions, motivation, and career aspirations. Small steps create an extensive journey forward that enables significant changes in your life. You discover an open road of exciting destinations that tempt you towards expansion. It marks an approach that redefines what is possible when you open your life outwardly. Creativity blooms as sunny skies emerge overhead. You enter a cycle of increasing opportunities that promotes good fortune.

15 Monday

You are on track to improving life, as experimental energy provides a new flavor as you breeze into a time of heightened sociability. Engaging with your broader circle of friends draws lighter power and an influx of potential into your social life. It brings forward-facing momentum that offers room to grow your tribe. Lively discussions harness manifestation's essence as bright ideas create opportunities to collaborate.

16 Tuesday

Research and resourcefulness help you enter a winning time of developing a dream project. It provides a passageway that gives you the green light to establish inspiring plans. With the wind beneath your wings, your social life bustles with new energy as you enter a productive cycle that offers both growth and possibility. Communication flows during brainstorming sessions that bring new ideas and projects to light.

17 Wednesday

You open a time that brings new elements into your life that offers growth and advancement. It is a fruitful time for deepening knowledge and gathering your resources as you embark on improving the foundations of your life. It provides a time of growing your world with an approach tinged with gold. You soon begin to see benefits emerging, giving you a good indication your star is rising.

18 Thursday

Life gets busy as you uncover an area that captures the essence of inspiration. It opens a trailblazing journey of working with your creativity and improving life. Increasing possibilities let you glide towards developing unique endeavors which come calling. It triggers ample time to connect with others and design projects. A whirlwind of activity in your socials sees life blossom under sunny skies.

19 Friday

Venus faces Neptune in a square designed to encourage you to take a look at your romantic goals. You may be seeking something out of reach in your love life. Looking at the filters you have in your love life helps dispel myths and fantasies. Unfulfilled sexual desires may intertwine with unrealistic fanciful expectations and conspire to build an area of denial. This planetary aspect encourages you to take down the castles in the sky and plant your feet in terra firma.

20 Saturday

Today's Sun conjunct Pluto transit increases your power and ability to influence beneficial outcomes in your life. Pluto sets up camp in Aquarius for the next 20 years. It brings the age of Pluto to Aquarius, a time of rising discoveries and scientific exploration. It will emphasize freedom-seeking and new ways of thinking, and this energy promotes developing creative approaches that heighten the potential. It is a welcome paradigm shift that offers to change the world.

21 Sunday

Changes ahead reboot your life and bring ample opportunity to grow your world. It kicks off an inspiring time that links up with social activities that ramp up potential in your life. A wellspring of magic courses through your social life, bringing improvement to valuable personal bonds. This wave of social engagement is a happy time shared with friends, which inspires positivity and joy.

22 Monday

You may feel under pressure and question the path ahead. New possibilities emerge, and tapping into this potential helps you get a new chapter off the ground. It launches your abilities higher to enact an active phase of growth and progression. Your willingness to explore options draws a pleasing result for your working life. It's about cultivating openness and being proactive about developing your life goals.

23 Tuesday

Venus settles into Capricorn to heighten security in your life. It brings rising energy to your ambitions, helping fuel change in your life. Upcoming changes help you create good headway in developing goals. It opens a prosperous cycle that lets you put your unique stamp on life. You take in an environment ripe with potential, and as your creativity rises to the challenge of advancing, you soon discover success. It places you in prime alignment for an upgrade worth your time.

24 Wednesday

A positive change opens to an enterprising time that offers expansion, happiness, and growth. It attracts an exciting journey that leaves you feeling enthusiastic about developing unique goals in your life. Plotting the path ahead lets you step towards progressing your knowledge and developing your skill set. It propels your abilities to the next level, and this advancement helps you build a rewarding path.

25 Thursday

The Full Moon is a chance to unwind and turn inward, as healing and therapeutically helpful influences wash over your awareness. Being receptive to the Moon's healing qualities offers room to resolve any sensitive areas clinging to your spirit. A healing and thoughtful vibe surround your life, promoting renewal and rejuvenation. It heals old wounds and creates a stable basis in your life. It helps you cut away from areas that are no longer relevant.

26 Friday

Rising optimism, let's luck sweep into your life and bring new possibilities to light. It illuminates a lighter and more social environment that expands your circle of friends. You discover plenty to celebrate as you set off in an exciting direction that releases the shadows and nurtures happiness in your world. It offers a lively and supportive environment that brings a sense of rejuvenation and renewal.

27 Saturday

Today, the Sun square Jupiter aspect draws golden vibrations into your life. It raises confidence and leaves you feeling optimistic about future potential. Notable changes ahead bring a more socially connected environment that enriches and delights. Fortune aligns to get a new source of happiness into your world. It lets you chart a course towards a stable and supportive landscape that offers expansion. It draws a busy time of engaging with your circle of friends.

28 Sunday

The Venus sextile Saturn transit today harmonizes personal bonds. It brings a levelheaded quality to your day-to-day interactions, promoting connection and balance. Creating space to plan for future growth brings the potential flowing into your life. Developments arise that bring sweet news into your life. It leads to an engaging time shared with friends.

<u>FEBRUARY</u>

Sun	Mon	Tue	Wed	Thu	Fri	Sat
				1	2 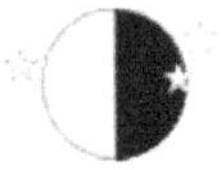	3
4	5	6	7	8	9 	10
11	12	13	14	15	16 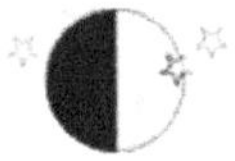	17
18	19	20	21	22	23	24 
25	26	27	28	29		

NEW MOON

SNOW MOON

29 Monday

Today's Venus trine Jupiter aspect draws beneficial outcomes into your social and personal life. Singles attract lively possibilities as they resonate with charm and magnetism. A lucky trine adds a dash of spontaneity to your life. Optimism and inspiration run wild as you reveal a social aspect that helps you grow and prosper. It migrates life away from troubles and brings a bright, sunny part that feels good for your soul. It opens a fortunate trend that attracts invitations ahead.

30 Tuesday

Improvements ahead open the door to new possibilities. Acting on instincts help you spot a diamond in the rough that bestows blessings upon your life. It opens a unique pathway of rising creativity that enables expansion as you tackle refreshing projects. Mapping out new goals creates stepping stones that build a meaningful way forward. It links you with growth as you discover new friends.

31 Wednesday

You enter a rising prospect cycle that opens the window to new endeavors. Good luck flows in when news arrives, which offers refreshing possibilities. It attracts new pathways that take you towards growth. It stirs up the winds of change, which helps you generate leads and improve circumstances. You can achieve gratifying results as you mark the journey ahead. It offers a transition that becomes an empowering time in your life.

1 Thursday

You are transitioning to a new chapter that offers broader benefits for your life. It lifts the lid on a trail that provides a wellspring of happiness as you connect with others in a supportive environment. Information and communication flow into your world, revealing exciting possibilities to mingle. It offers expansion to your circle of friends and improves the building blocks of your life.

FEBRUARY

2 Friday

Today, intuition sparks under the Mercury sextile with Neptune. You may feel more sensitive under this cosmic influence. Still, it also increases communitive abilities, which helps you dig deeper and gain information that lays below the surface of words and gestures. An insightful person shares advice and voices their thoughts with you. It brings a sense of support and an opportunity for collaboration with this person.

3 Saturday

A change of scenery ahead weaves a golden aspect through your romantic life. It brings thoughtful discussions that facilitate companionship. Inspiring changes expand your horizons and get unique possibilities for your utopian aspirations. Developing your love life becomes a strong focus as you discover room to deepen a personal bond. It begins a journey of rising possibilities that nurture stable foundations.

4 Sunday

Mercury ingress Aquarius has you seeking answers in your life; hot on the tail of this transit is Mercury conjunct Pluto, which adds intensity to personal communication. Probing questions reveal hidden answers today. Sharing thoughtful ideas fuels creative inspiration. It brings a potent time for manifesting fresh starts in your life. It brings a busy and active time of getting involved with new possibilities.

5 Monday

Important news reaches your inbox and opens an opportunity worth considering. Excitement and possibility run rife through this enterprising time of developing your talents in a unique direction. Advancing life towards new areas helps you gain a foothold on a path worth your time. It brings a change of pace that enables you to develop your talents and build your skill set. Designing the course ahead captures the essence of inspiration.

6 Tuesday

You are on a continuous cycle of growth and change. Expanding horizons let you explore areas that cultivate your talents. It brings an upgrade that offers progress as it rules a time of opportunity in your life. As you build upon your vision for future growth, you discover a rewarding environment that takes your talents to the next level. It initiates a time of rapid growth, which draws pleasing results.

7 Wednesday

You crack the code to a brighter phase when information emerges that feels heaven-sent. Opening your life up to new pathways helps you gather resources and embark on developing skills, and advance in a new area. It sparks a productive and lively environment that strongly emphasizes deepening knowledge. Dabbling in developing business ideas brings advancement into your life. You enter a valuable time of working with your abilities.

8 Thursday

The Mars sextile with Neptune today raises charisma and increases your appeal to others. This planetary aspect improves confidence as you radiate charm and find social interactions easy and flowing. It triggers a path of expanding opportunities, and being open to meeting new people expands your circle of friends. You discover there is room to spread your wings and embrace an active, connected environment that offers support and happiness.

9 Friday

A lighter chapter ahead helps you turn a corner and open a trend of renewal and rejuvenation. News arrives that lights an exciting journey of companionship and social opportunity. It lets you unpack a busy time brimming with new options. Happy developments see life moving forward towards a fortunate trend. It helps you develop a renewed sense of purpose as you connect with people who expand your life.

10 Saturday

Mercury Square Jupiter adds distraction which brings a lapse of concentration. You may find it challenging to follow conversations and stay on track as your mind tends to wander under this planetary aspect. Streamlining the demands on your time and weeding out distractions offers rising prospects that promote tangible results. Being methodical and working on the task at hand build stable foundations that usher in the terrific potential for your life.

11 Sunday

You lift the barriers and head towards change as you discover a lighter and happier phase in your personal life. It brings an engaging time of social interaction and friendly banter that adds playful energy to your romantic life. It brings a pleasing result that has you dreaming big about the possibilities as you deepen a bond with someone who offers enriching experiences of romance and connection.

FEBRUARY

12 Monday

A social gathering ahead becomes a focal point. It is a beautiful occasion that brings the opportunity to relax and engage with others. Sharing with friends lights the way forward towards expanding your life. You reveal a path that opens positive change as news arrives to bring a welcome boost. The wheels are in motion as new possibilities get a burst of fresh air to your surroundings.

13 Tuesday

Mars ingress Aquarius brings forward-thinking ideas that revolutionize the potential possible in your world. The Venus sextile Neptune brings a sense of anticipation into your life that has you looking forward to Valentine's Day. It offers big-sky dreaming as you indulge in romantic fantasies. Developing your romantic dreams becomes a priority, the start of a much larger theme that sprouts up in your life and will remain a significant focus for you this year.

14 Wednesday

Mars conjunct Pluto brings the drive and passion to your goals. It heightens sexual drive and desires, helping you nail your romantic goals today. Pouring your energy into your personal life draws supportive and thoughtful discussions. It brings a happy time that enables you to forge ahead in advance of life towards greener pastures. Romance and magic seamlessly weave around your life, connecting you with a meaningful journey worth your time.

15 Thursday

Information arrives that hits a sweet flavor in your life. It brings a beautiful journey of improving circumstances that connect with developing life outwardly. It attracts opportunities to mingle with your circle of friends. In a surprise move, someone from your past re-emerges to share news and catch up with you. It reveals a bright journey that has you feeling more connected, supported, and happy.

FEBRUARY

16 Friday

Venus sashays into Aquarius to raise the vibration in your romantic life. It showers harmonious beams over your social world, contributing to rising prospects in your life. It shines a light on a social aspect that connects you with someone who radiates your frequency. It promotes lively discussions and the sharing of ideas and thoughts. It reawakens you to a sense of connection that opens the floodgates to an enriching chapter.

17 Saturday

Rising possibilities cultivate change in your life. It brings an upgrade to your social life, and you discover a bright and breezy time shared with friends as you open the doors to a unique journey. It connects with a vibrant landscape that deepens bonds and links you with companionship, providing a wellspring of support in your life. Nurturing the path ahead promotes a pleasing result.

18 Sunday

You enter a chapter that bestows blessings over your social life. It lights a journey that promotes supportive discussions, activities, and engagement with your broader circle of friends. Positive energy soon ushers in an upgrade that feels exciting and expansive. It links you to kindred spirits who nurture trailblazing ideas that ignite passion and inspiration in your life.

19 Monday

Your social life heads toward a refreshing upswing, lighting up pathways of support and connectedness. It brings expansive horizons that offer to grow your circle of friends. Golden threads of possibility swirl around your social life. Sharing with valued companions replenishes your emotional tanks and draws security to the foundations around your life. It carries news on the winds of change.

20 Tuesday

You soon link up with kindred spirits who promote collaborative opportunities. You discover a group environment that helps you design goals and plan ambitious projects. Trailblazing options bring brainstorming sessions that encourage inspiration and creativity. Advancement is brewing in the background and soon opens the path forward. Your willingness to deepen your knowledge focuses on learning unique areas that come calling.

21 Wednesday

Leaning into your strengths enables a pleasing result. The path ahead clears, bringing a succession of positive outcomes that have you feeling optimistic about your career life. Focusing on the building blocks and setting your intentions enables you to make the most of the changes ahead. As you deepen your knowledge and advance your skills, you extend your reach into new areas worth your time. A new phase soon cranks up the level of growth in your career.

22 Thursday

Venus conjunct Mars increases sexual charisma and drive. It heightens intimacy and yearning for exceptional bonding. If you crave romantic downtime today, you know which planets are involved in the passion which propels you forward towards creating magic and mayhem in your love life. Sharing thoughts with someone compatible brings touching moments that feel heartwarming. It lifts the lid on changes that nourish your spirit and inspire your mind.

23 Friday

Thanks to Mercury slipping into Pisces to increase your thought processes, you receive a boost of mental clarity and an uptick in analytical reasoning abilities today. You discover a blossoming journey ahead enables top results. Attention to detail and avoiding distractions brings a top result. You enter a rising aspect regarding your career path. It does get a positive environment that ushers in a busy time. Productivity shines brightly, and this brings terrific feedback.

24 Saturday

A Full moon in Virgo draws understanding, clarity, and insight. It offers a broader overview of your life, nurturing a therapeutic and healing environment. This Full Moon is a time for focusing on cultivating a sentimental and contemplative vibe that releases outworn energy. Afterward, it places you in the proper alignment to grow your life and move towards new possibilities. A personal breakthrough launches a fresh chapter in your world that brings stable foundations into view.

25 Sunday

Venus Square Jupiter's planetary aspect brings a fun-loving vibe into your social life. Good fortune, sharing, and caring with friends light an engaging path that nurtures well-being and happiness in your life. Opportunity comes knocking and brings expansion into your life. It marks a time that improves foundations and enhances security in your world. This ticket to a way forward nurtures an upward trend worth developing.

26 Monday

Your willingness to explore new possibilities draws a pleasing result for your life. Refreshing options bring pathways to growth. A highly productive chapter ahead is a source of great inspiration in your world. It brings a time of working with your skills and nurturing your abilities. You blaze a trail towards refining your skills and growing your talents as you extend your reach in a new direction.

27 Tuesday

Mars square Jupiter brings positive energy, heightening confidence and enthusiasm for life. You are the captain of your ship; growing your world sparks a journey that leaves you feeling optimistic. A sense of wanderlust drives your vision, and you chart a course towards an exciting vista of possibilities. It lets you break free from restrictive patterns as possibilities to improve your circumstances light a path. It brings rocket fuel for inspiration as you get busy planning goals.

28 Wednesday

Sun conjunct Mercury brings news and communication. It ushers in an expressive social aspect that cultivates lively discussions, engagement, and sharing with friends and companions. It illustrates the benefits of creative thinking, as innovative possibilities inspire new leads for potential development. Investing your energy in promoting your talents brings a journey of self-development and growth.

29 Thursday

Jupiter's positive vibration seals that deal on a Mercury-infused forward-thinking day. Mercury in sextile with Jupiter offers an ideal opportunity to think about the future and engage in brainstorming as you plan future goals. It brings an option ripe for development that moves you in alignment with the person you are becoming. Plotting a course towards developing your life kicks off an ambitious venture worth your time.

<u>MARCH</u>

Sun	Mon	Tue	Wed	Thu	Fri	Sat
					1	2
3 	4	5	6	7	8	9
10 	11	12	13	14	15	16
17 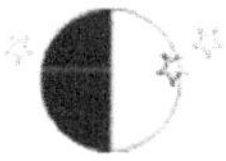	18	19	20	21	22	23
24	25 	26	27	28	29	30
31						

Aries

NEW MOON

WORM MOON

MARCH

1 Friday

One of astrology's most favored transits lights up your day. In sextile with Jupiter, the Sun brings golden beams of positivity into your life. You touch down on a landscape filled with options and possibilities. New potential emerges that opens a gate forward. It brings a productive chapter that offers room to develop your abilities as you take on a new assignment that showcases your talents. It brings a dynamic environment that illuminates working with your gifts.

2 Saturday

You discover a chance to design new goals close to your heart. Being in charge of the path ahead brings a gust of fresh air into your surroundings and promotes new foundations. Developing a passion project becomes a strong emphasis, and this endeavor creates forward momentum that propels you towards an exciting time shared with like-minded people. Brainstorming sessions draw creative possibilities that inspire change.

3 Sunday

Venus Square Uranus brings restless energy that offers deliberate you from constraints that keep you tied down and feeling limited. You feel called to liberate yourself from restrictive circumstances and patterns. It brings a spontaneous element that promotes refreshing adventures that change your day-to-day routines. It cracks the code to a brighter chapter that tempts you to engage proactively with life. It lets you be self-expressive, engaging, and happy.

4 Monday

An influx of possibilities brings new options into your life. It gets you involved with opportunities that help you develop your skills and nurture your dreams. A change of scenery brings choices that fuel inspiration and drive. Increasing motivation enables you to climb the ladder towards developing ventures worth your time. It opens a lucrative path that advances goals to the next level. It allows you to unleash your talents in a new area.

5 Tuesday

Being confident, enthusiastic, and capable draws rising potential into your career path. A new approach looms overhead and enables you to advance towards a brighter chapter in your working life. It does bring a journey that inspires change and leaves you feeling motivated to nail your career goals. It brings a clean slate of potential into your working life. It brings rising opportunities that crack the code to a brighter chapter.

6 Wednesday

Opportunity comes knocking and opens a journey that inspires progress around your life. It captures the essence of wanderlust as you develop a dream that promotes happiness. As you design the path and create progress around your life, you build more balanced foundations that offer heightened security and stability. Life opens to a vibrant landscape that redefines what you thought possible in your world. It does lift the lid on an inspiring environment ripe with blessings.

7 Thursday

You enter a joyful, breezy time chock-full of opportunities to engage with your circle of friends. It brings happy experiences and moments that promote bonding. Thoughtful discussions bring a creative project to light. Collaboration, brainstorming, and working with others to achieve your chosen destination become a strong emphasis. Designing dreams and spending quality time with kindred spirits draws laughter and joy.

8 Friday

Exploring avenues of growth in your life enables you to head on an upswing. Launching towards developing new areas connects you with others who help you create steady progress as you design goals and nurture your life. It brings a significant time of discovery that enables you to navigate the path and open the trail to excellent options which grow your experience. It provides the right environment to usher in unique possibilities.

9 Saturday

A Mars square Uranus planetary transit hits a freedom-loving vibe in time for Saturday night adventures. It brings a restlessness that seeks expression as you break free from constraints and head towards a liberating time shared with friends. You unearth an option that connects you with a vibrant side of life. It highlights a community environment that lets you connect with like-minded people. Life-affirming invitations connect you with kindred spirits.

10 Sunday

Mercury ingress Aries offers improvement as newfound energy and drive help you accomplish a great deal. Notable changes ahead draw growth and progression. It puts you in contact with someone who supports and nurtures your life. It enables you to ride a wave of hopeful energy as you become more involved with your social life. Pouring time into developing social bonds brings supportive discussions and thoughtful dialogues.

11 Monday

Venus ingress Pisces is a favorable transit for your love life. It harmonizes emotional bonds and elevates potential in your personal life. An emphasis on your romantic life gives you a nudge in the right direction, enabling you to spend more time improving your love life. Developing interpersonal bonds draws an expressive and happy time. You ease into a time that offers improvement. You settle into an environment that brings all kinds of benefits into your world.

12 Tuesday

You have lots happening on the schedule soon. Advancement results from your quest as an emphasis on improving your life opens opportunities to help you move upwards and achieve greatness. Working towards your vision for the future draws a pleasing result. A positive influence raises confidence and enables you to build a concrete path forward. Taking advantage of all the options ahead rekindles vitality. Life leads to a fantastic time that expands the boundaries of your life.

13 Wednesday

As you step out on a journey of increasing possibilities, life becomes lighter and sweeter. A creative venture becomes a hot topic of conversation in your circle of friends. It activates a group environment that nurtures your talents as you contribute knowledge and share your skills with others. It brings an enterprising time that keeps you on your toes. You enter a vital time for being productive, which enhances project development.

14 Thursday

Life brings opportunities to shift your focus toward growth and advancement. Improvement ahead boosts confidence and brings lighter energy. It promotes a time that nurtures well-being and harmony in your life. As you improve your bottom line, you step out on a journey that offers a social connection. It brings the right environment to share with friends engagingly. A new realm of options in your life draws dividends.

MARCH

15 Friday

Life is ready to offer new opportunities that open an upward trend. It brings a socially involved time shared with friends. Indeed, lively conversations boost energy and bring excitement as you launch towards expanding your circle. You attract companionship, which nourishes your life. It reawakens possibilities as you enjoy a vibrant landscape of potential. Nurturing this time draws stable foundations as old challenges melt away.

16 Saturday

Upcoming changes open the door to a bright chapter in your life. It ignites a time that offers unique friendships and a chance to participate in social and community activities. You touch down in a supportive environment that provides room to grow your talents. Working with your creativity promotes rising prospects that merge with inspiration to facilitate developing your life outwardly.

17 Sunday

Sun conjunct Neptune transit increases intuition and empathy today. It brings an appropriate time to reflect and contemplate future dreams and goals. Curious changes ahead unlock possibilities for romance and companionship. A social aspect lights up your calendar with news, invitations, and opportunities to mingle. Good news arrives with a flurry and is a cause for celebration. As you chart a course towards a mesmerizing destination, your love life picks up speed.

18 Monday

You enter a time of rejuvenation that smooths over the rough edges of your life. It promotes healing and helps you sweep away aspects that are no longer relevant. Moving away from the outworn areas, gently shift your focus towards developing new goals for your life. Setting intentions blends with various manifestations to help open the path ahead. It brings a journey of discovery to the crux of the progression ahead.

19 Tuesday

Putting your dreams on the front burner ignites creativity and helps you develop viable solutions for your life. Discipline and commitment draw satisfying results as you get busy creating new possibilities and taking action towards enhancing your life. You tap into a path of promise and potential that develops a broad theme of expanding horizons in your life. It does take you on a journey of plenty and prosperity.

20 Wednesday

News arrives, which grows your world and sparks the journey that has you feeling optimistic about the rising prospects in your life. You land in a productive and active environment ripe with new leads. Fanning the flames of inspiration attracts creative fuel, allowing room to nurture your talents. Growing your skills sees you launch your abilities successfully and develop an area worth your time. Your perseverance and willingness to broaden your search help you turn a corner.

21 Thursday

Sun sextile Pluto transit increases your drive. You feel more determined and purposeful than usual, which helps you achieve your goals today. Rising prospects attract bright blessings into your life. A great deal of potential is coming into your surroundings; it triggers a productive phase of expansion, prosperity, and growth. Developing plans opens the door to a time of advancement and possibility. It brings progress which helps you move onward with a renewed sense of purpose.

22 Friday

The transit of Mars in Pisces reduces issues in your life as this favorable aspect draws good fortune and rising prospects. It elevates financial possibilities, leading to a winning path forward. Increasing opportunities ahead bring a positive outcome that grows your life. Researching various options attracts new leads to your career path. The more you work on developing your vision for future growth, the greater the success.

23 Saturday

You enter a time for news and activities promoting positive aspects of your life. It helps you cultivate new adventures that bring a lighter and more spontaneous note into your world. Being open to change helps grow your life in a unique direction. It gives you a chance to deepen a bond that inspires your life with vital energy. You enjoy sharing thoughts and networking with friends who grow your life. It brings a lighter, happier time of nurturing your social life.

24 Sunday

Venus sextile Jupiter raises confidence as good fortune flows into your life. It introduces a lucky aspect that improves finances, relationships, and circumstances. You discover the right avenue to channel your restless energy into developing. You can cast your net of dreams expansively as a comprehensive approach enables you to make the most of the options. It brings a busy time that sees your circle of friends expanding.

25 Monday

A Full Moon brings healing into your surroundings to wash away the outworn areas and soothe your spirit with a therapeutic influence. Taking a step back from sensitive areas provides a broader perspective that nourishes a healing effect. Removing outworn energy resolves sensitive areas and helps you move towards greener pastures. New possibilities spring to life and open a blossoming path forward. It does bring a time of significant personal growth and advancement.

26 Tuesday

You discover the correct elements to thrive in a unique landscape that promotes skill development. Refining your abilities draws advancement. It lets you take on an enterprising area that offers rising prospects. You soon build stable foundations which heighten the security around your life. These new options become a catalyst for growth which helps you climb the rungs to a successful outcome. A curious assignment comes calling and lights up development and learning areas.

27 Wednesday

You hone in on a productive environment that offers progress. It brings a busy time that draws stability into your working life. As you get busy developing your career path, advancement is looming, bringing a pleasing outcome. You receive recognition, which makes you feel valued in the workplace. Things are on the move this week, getting fruitful results you can appreciate. Growth, advancement, and progress are within reach.

28 Thursday

A currency of information flows into your life, giving you news and options to help you make an informed decision. It begins a journey that eclipses the past by opening your life to new experiences. It touches all areas of your life as it earmarks remarkable opportunities for growth ahead. It helps you forge new friendships and expand your life outwardly. It nurtures a happy environment. Working towards your dreams offers tangible results that promote advancement in your life.

29 Friday

Staying open to new possibilities, people, and opportunities bodes well for your life. It opens a journey that feeds creativity and leaves you optimistic about future potential. A major topic of discussion shared with friends opens a way worth growing. It brings opportunities to mingle that uplift your world. Circulating with like-minded people brings happiness and companionship to the forefront of your life.

30 Saturday

Opportunity comes knocking, bringing news that sees the return of optimism and happiness. It helps you transition to a social aspect that leaves you feeling joyful. You are in your most pleasing element as you share thoughtful conversations with friends. Pursuing your goals brings a positive influence that brightens your mood. Supportive friends bring insight and sharing into your life, offering a bright and breezy time ahead.

31 Sunday

Curious changes ahead bring your focus towards developing a journey of meaning in your life. It connects to magic and opportunity that nurtures growth and rising prospects. Lightness and momentum tempt you in a way that brings new adventures as you head towards transformation. It offers a soul journey that helps you move in alignment with your spiritual side. Deepening your knowledge and learning a new area draws a pleasing result.

<u>APRIL</u>

Sun	Mon	Tue	Wed	Thu	Fri	Sat
	1	2	3	4	5	6
7	8	9	10	11	12	13
14	15	16	17	18	19	20
21	22	23	24	25	26	27
28	29	30				

NEW MOON

Pink Moon

April

1 Monday

Mercury turns Retrograde on April Fools' Day, bringing a little joke from the heavens. It is a time that stalls progress as miscommunication and mixed signals are more prevalent in your social life. You face a crossroads ahead that lets you remove the outworn areas of your life. Acting on a hunch moves you in alignment with a happier aspect. It rules a time of rising intuition that guides you forward correctly towards new goals.

2 Tuesday

It is a time of transformation in your life; it does bring upheaval as you re-evaluate the path ahead with a new lens of perception. Priorities change, and soul-searching brings unique insights. Tweaking and refining goals help create the right environment to launch new projects. It promotes a more creative and expressive journey forward that hits a sweet note in your life. Rebuilding your vision for future growth renews your sense of optimism.

3 Wednesday

Venus conjunct Neptune brings rising possibilities for singles to find a romantic partner. It also offers advancement for couples as a favorable influence nurtures growth. Necessary changes ahead have you moving towards a fresh start. You welcome a surge of new options that bring an optimistic vibe into your world. It offers a time that connects you with magic and opportunity. It gets personal growth as it takes you towards an abundant environment.

4 Thursday

You see changes in your creativity, enabling you to take your talents in a unique direction. Doing research unearths new leads that help you excel in growing your skills. It brings a productive time where you concentrate on increasing life and forging your path forward. Trusting your instincts will let your intuition be your guide as you open your life to unique side trails that call to grow your experience.

5 Friday

Venus ingress Aries brings a thoughtful aspect that helps you rediscover your passion and creativity. It places the spotlight on nurturing hobbies and growing interests in your life. Fanning the flames of your inspiration brings creative fuel that heads you towards success. You land in a productive and active environment ripe with possibility. New options ahead advance your goals. It brings a progressive and prosperous path that nurtures your talents and grows your skills.

6 Saturday

Venus sextile Pluto adds depth, meaning, and curiosity. It has you wanting to peel back the layers and discover what lies beneath the surface of everyday life. You may feel a restless element in your life calling your wild heart. Staying true to the energy that seeks expression in your life offers a spontaneous feature that brings a shift of priorities. Letting your emotions guide you forward enables you to nurture foundations as you head towards a purposeful chapter.

7 Sunday

Being open to meeting new people helps you shake off heavy vibes and enter a new chapter of growth in your social life. A piece of your puzzle reveals as you deepen a bond that offers curious changes which promote companionship. Finding the missing element in your life helps unlock an incredible chapter of personal growth. It enables you to push back the barriers and embrace a more connected future.

8 Monday

Understanding the broader picture of options surrounding your life cracks the code for a meaningful and well-designed journey forward. Focusing on stable and balanced foundations supports well-being and happiness. You can soon close the book on hardship and embrace a lighter path. Expanding your life into unique areas offers a positive shift that attracts possibilities worth your time. Designing your life draws progression and aligns you towards achieving a positive result.

9 Tuesday

The more you dabble with life, the more life meets you with new possibilities worth your time and energy. Incoming news brings an opportunity that bears fruit as you take steps toward building a venture that offers room to grow your life. As you dip into this new avenue of possibility, you discover kindred spirits who share similar goals. It brings a group environment that connects you with like-minded individuals who draw insightful discussions and supportive dialogues.

10 Wednesday

Mars conjunct Saturn ignites determination and drive, which helps you excel in the workplace. An opportunity ahead fosters rising optimism. You get involved in learning an area that holds water and revs up the success rate for your career. As you create a bridge towards growing your dreams, you discover a venture that opens the door wide. Gaining traction on achieving your goals becomes a strong focus. You keep forging ahead until you accomplish the rightful outcome.

11 Thursday

A curious assignment ahead lights up pathways of creativity and artistic expression. It brings a chance to take your gifts to a broader audience and link with a group environment that nurtures fresh possibilities in your life. Getting involved with kindred spirits brings the chance to cultivate friendships in a social setting. Communication flows as you spend time with others. It speaks of a refreshing change of pace that sees your social life gaining momentum.

12 Friday

Getting involved with your social life draws benefits as you move towards an ample expressive, lively, and engaging time. You soon brew up a storm of possibility with treasured companions who inspire creative ideas and offer a chance to design projects worth developing. An option ahead brings collaboration opportunities, which translates to a fresh chapter in your social life. It lets you chart a course towards improving your situation.

13 Saturday

Taking time to plan the steps brings wide-ranging benefits into your life as your insights and creativity guide you towards the right environment. You discover a lucky climate that has you dreaming big about future possibilities. It opens the way toward a productive and lively journey offering positive change. Life becomes more manageable as you discover a journey of ease and plenty. It nurtures a creative time that draws expansion as you work with your gifts to achieve growth.

14 Sunday

Today emphasizes developing your home life and building security around your world. It opens life up to an exciting flavor as you get busy setting goals that promote happy foundations. It offers valuable time to nurture your dreams on the home front. The conditions are superb to gain traction on your larger goals. It paves the way forward toward rising prospects. You open a highly productive cycle that brings new possibilities into your life.

15 Monday

Being in sync with your vision for future growth aligns you with developing your talents. Refining abilities let you feel more in control over the path ahead. As you focus on the journey, not the destination, you discover that life rewards on many levels—preparation, planning, and strategizing provide intriguing leads. You hatch potential dreams and nurture them with loving attention to detail. It lets you emerge a winner as you embark on an enchanting time of discovery.

16 Tuesday

Becoming involved with growing your life brings progress and optimism into your world. It creates a stable foundation that illuminates new possibilities that help you craft your vision for future growth. As you journey towards developing a long-held goal, you begin to feel more hopeful about the rising prospects in your life. It helps you focus on meaningful areas that inspire your life and grow your abilities. An undercurrent of unique potential brings pathways and possibilities.

17 Wednesday

You hit a home run and head for a winning streak when discovering a treasure trove of opportunities ahead. You receive news that brings a boost into your world. It has a powerful effect, providing you with a new landscape of options. It draws a happy shift forward that lets you release areas that have caused blocks and lack of progress. Refining and streamlining your situation amplifies potential and enables you to turn a corner and head towards growth.

18 Thursday

You open a compelling route forward as several enticing options cross your path. It brings stable foundations that let you forge ahead towards enriching your life with new possibilities. Attractive options along bring a bounty of potential into your life. It generates excitement and progression as it offers an efficient and effective phase for growing your goals. It brings productivity, busyness, and expansion. Resourceful planning helps you plot a course towards growth.

19 Friday

Mars sextile Jupiter transit makes you feel confident today. This planetary aspect is ideal for tackling complex tasks because there is an excellent chance of success. This transit has a well-earned reputation for good luck as it increases optimism and initiative and brings a willingness to take calculated risks. It lets you take on an enterprising area that offers rising prospects. Life becomes a blur of refreshing options that keep you motivated and optimistic about future possibilities.

20 Saturday

Mars sextile Uranus offers unique ideas that help you think outside the box to obtain innovative solutions. Uranus places the focus on rebellion, liberation, and freedom. It adds a dash of spontaneity to your life today. You head towards an active time of engaging with your social life. It brings outings and opportunities that feel adventurous. Keeping life vivid and dynamic draws happy times that uplift the mood. You find flavor by adding variety to your life.

21 Sunday

Jupiter's conjunct Uranus transit provides surprises and sudden opportunities. Good news lands in a flurry of excitement. New possibilities arrive to keep your focus on expanding life forward towards greener pastures. Exploring leads and researching options helps you come up with a winning trajectory. It provides you with an approach that lets you chase your vision for future growth. You soon build stable foundations that heighten the security in your life.

22 Monday

A new project arrives and getting involved with this area lets you put your personal touch on things. Artistic expression and creativity are on the rise, opening pathways that grow your talents. A significant assignment boosts your spirit as it opens a clear path forward for your abilities. Working with your capabilities and developing life in new areas brings good fortune. It helps you create tangible results that guide a chapter of discovery and movement.

23 Tuesday

The Full Moon draws a healing and therapeutic influence into your life. Past struggles fade away as a healing effect sweeps away outworn energy. You head towards a time that favors growth; a crossroads ahead brings a decision that helps you cut troublesome aspects. It brings improvement that sets the tone for developing stable foundations that enrich your world. Exploring leads brings change and progression that marks a turning point.

24 Wednesday

Being open to change facilitates expansion as it opens life up to new options. It gives you the green light to link up with developing cutting-edge initiatives that deepen your knowledge. Actively exploring pathways around your life attracts new opportunities worth your time. It culminates in a turning point that cracks the code to grow your life outwardly. As you dig deeper into your goals, you discover new pathways of inspiration.

25 Thursday

Mercury turns direct, improving personal bonds and opening the path to growing your social life. It brings a happy chapter that puts you in contact with kindred spirits. Lively discussions give you the green light to get the ball rolling on developing your social life. It sets the tone for an exciting time shared with friends and companions. Life becomes more active and engaging; it opens the way toward rising prospects.

26 Friday

News arrives that opens the door wide as it brings new information. It offers a turning point that helps you create headway on designing the path ahead. Under this positive influence, new goals take shape; it promotes a progressive and prosperous time that cultivates change in your life. It teams you up with others who share trailblazing discussions in a group environment. Nurturing this interconnected web of support draws happiness.

27 Saturday

A new attitude and rising confidence bring a chance to step out and enjoy growing a path that offers room to revolutionize the potential possible in your world. It rules a way of expansion that brings people into your life. Expanding your network of friends brings goodness to the top of your life. It moves you towards a more lively environment. Networking and mingling see you move in circles that offer expansion for your life.

28 Sunday

A purposeful push towards developing new goals paves the way toward progress and increasing possibility in your life. Manifesting happiness is on the agenda; it cracks open a journey of kinship and companionship that bodes well for your romantic life. Being open to all that life can offer brings improvement ahead. Opportunity comes knocking when good news arrives with a flurry of excitement. It ushers in an impressive aspect that fosters growth and happiness.

May

Sun	Mon	Tue	Wed	Thu	Fri	Sat
			1	2	3	4
5	6	7	8	9	10	11
12	13	14	15	16	17	18
19	20	21	22	23	24	25
26	27	28	29	30	31	

NEW MOON

FLOWER MOON

29 Monday

Venus in Taurus brings a harmonizing influence that offers grounded foundations for your social life. It helps you approach relationships and life warmly, earthy and balanced manner. Today, a Mars conjunct Neptune aspect raises potential in your romantic life; it has you dreaming big about the possibilities. You begin to take the first steps on a personal journey that holds meaning. Pouring your energy into growing your life draws a happy result.

30 Tuesday

Mars lands in Aries, and this raises confidence. It's time to go big and be bold. Your best qualities will enter the spotlight and gain recognition soon. It brings a page-turning chapter when the path ahead clears. Moving beyond your current comfort level expands your horizons in an exciting direction. News arrives, which offers room to grow your skills. It brings a time of developing talents and increasing the potential around your world.

1 Wednesday

Today's aspect could see a flare-up of jealousy or possessiveness. Your romantic partner may feel threatened by heightened social activities and invitations flowing into your life. Take time to support and boost confidence to help offset the Venus square Pluto aspect. Being aware of these fears' dynamics helps keep relationships healthy and balanced. Open sharing releases the heaviness and transforms your situation into a brighter chapter.

2 Thursday

Pluto is the modern ruler of Scorpio; it symbolizes how we experience power, renewal, rebirth, and mysterious or subconscious forces. This Pluto retrograde phase allows you to dive deep and explore inner realms and darker aspects of your personality ordinarily hidden from view. Understanding your psyche deeper provides access to the forces driving your personality.

3 Friday

Mars sextile Pluto transit increases energy in the workplace. No job is too small as you take on the lot and work towards your vision. Working effectively and efficiently towards your goals hold you in good stead. You no longer feel as though you are treading water; you begin to see the kind of progress you have been working tirelessly to achieve. It opens avenues that encourage expansion.

4 Saturday

News arrives, which draws a productive time as it connects you with a phase of social engagement. A situation you become involved with begins to move forward, attracting expansion and growth. It offers a time that reshapes your social life as it encourages change and evolution in your world. It draws an engaging time of social interaction that leads to happy encounters. It offers fertile ground to explore developing unique ideas and creative inspiration with kindred spirits.

5 Sunday

A lovely change enables you to nurture more personal aspects. It helps create space to build a balanced and grounded energy around your home life. An area you seek to develop brings enriching and meaningful prospects into your life. You feel that life has more substance and significance as you concentrate on goals that hold the most significant meaning around your situation. Creating more balance and stability draws a pleasing result.

6 Monday

Improvements are bound for your life as you benefit significantly from events on the horizon. You no longer feel like you are treading water as you sail toward new adventures. It offers a fresh start that improves stability and happiness. The tide turns in your favor, enabling choices and decisions to trigger a path that takes you towards rising prospects. It draws a replenishing vibe that brings renewal and rejuvenation.

7 Tuesday

Sun sextile Saturn transit lends patience and perseverance; it enables you to gain traction on achieving challenging goals in your life. As you gain traction on advancing your working goals, it promotes a time of growth and stability in your working environment. As your abilities head towards advancement, it draws a productive environment that sees you working innovatively and effectively to grow your career trajectory.

8 Wednesday

There is plenty ahead to keep you feeling inspired. It brings a more active environment that shifts your focus towards developing new goals. It helps you snag a choice opportunity that advances your talents and draws rising prospects into your life. It takes you on a journey that offers growth, learning, and wisdom. Rising good fortune kicks off a cycle of prosperity and potential. Your pioneering spirit blazes a trail towards an exciting destination.

9 Thursday

Opportunities in the workplace draw an active time that offers growth and prosperity. It opens your life to a broader bounty of possibility as an opportunity comes knocking, and this gives you an exciting sign that things are shifting forward in your life. Newfound motivation fuels inspiration and enables you to launch into a chapter of gain and progression. Life is ripe with remarkable possibilities worthy of development.

10 Friday

News arrives, which helps you make exceptional progress on developing the path ahead. It boosts positive energy and offers an encouraging vibe that promotes expansion. You discover creative people in your broader circle of friends; a networking opportunity aligns your energy with lively discussions and thoughtful dialogues. It releases the shadows and removes the cobwebs. An undercurrent of unique potential helps you thrive in a vibrant and dynamic environment.

11 Saturday

Expanding horizons brings news and information. Communication arrives to tempt you out in the broader community. It aligns you with the direction of growing your social life. It connects you with a social aspect that draws happiness and harmony into your surroundings. Sharing thoughtful discussions with kindred spirits nurtures well-being. It offers a time of insightful dialogues that illustrates increasing stability and balance in your world.

12 Sunday

Beautiful changes are emerging around your home and family life. It offers a chance to mingle with people who support your growth and evolution. Connecting with your social life draws an active time of nurturing happiness. Trailblazing conversations lead to the development of new ideas. Dabbling in your interests shines a light on nurturing creativity in your life. It secures foundations that draw stability and balance into your surroundings.

13 Monday

A positive influence from the Sun conjunct Uranus planetary aspect brings a boost that sparks new options. It opens a journey that holds blessings and offers to revolutionize the potential possible in your world. The Venus sextile Saturn transit today increases your need for company, and you may yearn to connect with friends. It lets you make strides towards improving life by expanding your circle of friends.

14 Tuesday

News arrives, tinged with the currency of change. It imbues a sense of purpose as it offers a driven chapter of growth in your life. You hit upon a positive trend that resonates with your spirit. It brings a colorful chapter that expands life outwardly with opportunities to socialize. It lets you wear your rebel clothes and embrace an adventurous time of expansion. It brings opportunities for freedom, growth, and happiness. Riding a wave of inspiration carries you along on the winds of change.

15 Wednesday

Mercury settles into Taurus; your thinking is down to earth, balanced, and grounded. Life brims with possibility as you chart a course towards growing your working life. It brings tangible results that heighten security and offer rich rewards for your life. Expanding your career path lets you cross the threshold and settle into a more secure environment. Good luck figures prominently as you launch towards developing areas that catch your interest.

16 Thursday

Life takes on a meandering pace as you settle into a landscape of potential and possibility. A positive influence ahead transitions you towards learning a new area. It brings remarkable changes that give you the green light to nurture your abilities and grow your talents. It lets you find your groove as you expand life outwardly. You discover a lead that lays the groundwork for a stable basis from which to grow your world. A new project overhead comes calling.

17 Friday

Information arrives that opens the door to a fresh start. It marks a new beginning that brings a shift towards expansion as it extends the borders of your life. It offers a social aspect that shines a light on nurturing friendship. Thoughtful conversations allow you to join forces with a co-conspirator who brings the gift of companionship. Sharing thoughts and ideas draw well-being and harmony into your world. It taps into a creative vibe that cracks the code to a happy chapter.

18 Saturday

Venus teams up with Uranus to add a dash of spontaneity to your social/personal life. Another conjunct occurs between the Sun and Jupiter, adding lightness and momentum to your life. A social aspect brings an environment ripe with potential. Refreshing options allow you to step out on an enterprising journey which helps you gain a foothold on a lighter path that offers your life companionship. It brings a time of growing your experience in a remarkable direction.

19 Sunday

News arrives that highlights a path of creativity, self-expression, and possibility. You discover a richly abundant journey that lights a way forward in your life. It brings collaboration and progress that draws rising prospects into your social life. It connects you with a thoughtful and trailblazing time of sharing insights and ideas with someone who understands your take on life. Getting in touch with your dreams helps you cross the threshold to developing your world outwardly.

20 Monday

A transformational aspect has a profound effect on your spirit. It offers to heal and nurture well-being as you improve the foundations and nurture the possibilities in your world. It encourages you to push the barriers back and head towards change. A new role on offer inspires a great deal of excitement. The conditions for growth ripen, and you achieve more stability and progression. Well-crafted ideas underscore the essence of magic and manifestation in your world.

21 Tuesday

You cook up a good brew and manifest your happiness by focusing on your goals and priorities. Cultivating your creativity adds the fuel of inspiration to your life, which enables you to grow your circumstances and develop your dreams. It helps you promote progress as you create new projects and launch your star towards growth. An upward trend ahead offers room to advance your skills and abilities. The winds of change breathe fresh air into your surroundings.

22 Wednesday

The Sun trine Pluto aspect increases your desire to gain power and drive your ambitious streak to greater heights. It is a significant time that empowers growth as you achieve a lofty goal. The power of manifestation leads the way toward more substantial transformation, which opens the floodgates to rising prospects. It lets you strike gold as you turn the corner and chart a course towards growth. You head to an extended time that reinvents the potential possible in your world.

23 Thursday

Today's Venus conjunct Jupiter aspect is a positive sign for your social life. Venus harmonizes bonds and draws a dreamy vibe when she forms a sextile with Neptune. The Venus ingress into Gemini draws balanced energy, which nurtures your romantic and social life. As Gemini adds lightness and harmony to conversations, Venus is the perfect companion which links up to growth around your tribe. Conversations are light, breezy, and fun, bringing a boost to your life.

24 Friday

Unexpected developments bring a happy surprise into your life. It orients you towards growing your social life and gives you time for fun. Friends and companionship energize your social life, and this trend continues as you infuse bonds with an optimistic and upbeat approach. Confidence rises, and your ability to attract people into your circle becomes magnetic. It brings an influx of messages and communication that lets you know you are appreciated and valued.

25 Saturday

Venus trine Pluto brings an increasing drive that adds intensity as it has you focusing on developing future goals sooner rather than later. Jupiter's ingress Gemini is a favorable planetary aspect that promotes harmony. It brings fresh air into your surroundings and a light and breezy vibe that feels good for your soul. Positive changes open a journey of thoughtful discussions and lively moments. It marks a time of fun and possibility that brings new ideas to light.

26 Sunday

Working with your gifts offers a calming influence that releases stress and nurtures well-being. Rebalancing your energy by focusing on the basics in your life draws harmony and happiness. A positive trend emerges that brings a busy time of shaping goals and launching your star higher towards a new vision. Opportunities ahead expand your life and attract a pleasing outcome that rewards you on many levels. A forward-facing focus helps you achieve the best results possible.

27 Monday

An enriching time shared with others provides a fresh start on many levels. It reawakens you to a broader world of potential. Life becomes smoother as new possibilities emerge to grow the potential in your world. It brings a refreshing aspect that focuses on social goals. It brings invitations to participate in communal celebrations and social engagement. As you negotiate a busy environment, you make the most of this time by sharing with friends.

28 Tuesday

With Mercury in sextile with Saturn, communication skills are rising. Enhanced clarity and mental insight help you understand more significant concepts, thought processes, and ideas with ease today. This cosmic enhancement enables you to step beyond traditional learning and take your studies/working life to the next level. Information ahead shines a light on an area worth your time and energy. It brings an exciting change of pace which opens the path forward.

29 Wednesday

A lucky break brings a valuable opportunity that feeds your soul. It benefits your life on several levels as energy improves, and you feel happier and more optimistic about the potential in your world. An endeavor you develop will progress and keep life humming as you engage in projects and areas that capture your inspiration. Your ability to work towards a plan produces an abundant harvest that enriches your life. Keeping goals focused draws a high return into your life.

30 Thursday

You will have an opportunity to develop an area that offers improvement. Working on your goals will see an influx of favorable signs that let you know you can create progress if you focus on achieving your best. Planning and tweaking projects will offer rising results that bring valuable rewards flowing into your life. Your willingness to be adaptable and pivot at a moment's notice will come in handy when surprise news lands in your lap.

June

Sun	Mon	Tue	Wed	Thu	Fri	Sat
						1
2	3	4	5	6 	7	8
9	10	11	12	13	14 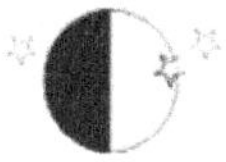	15
16	17	18	19	20	21	22 
23	24	25	26	27	28 	29
30						

NEW MOON

STRAWBERRY MOON

31 Friday

Mercury and Uranus form a positive aspect that heightens mental abilities. Increasing mental stimulation promotes fresh ideas in your life today. Technology, messages, and communication all spark inspiration and foster possibilities for future development. Life picks up steam, and invitations arrive, which increases overall enthusiasm and energy. Your motivation sparkles brightly, confidence increases, and you thrive in a connected environment.

1 Saturday

Jupiter trine Pluto transit improves confidence and brings a powerful influence that helps you exert your power to gain control over developing your vision for future growth. You will feel more in control over the passage ahead and be able to use your mastery to obtain positive results in your life. You are ready to forge a unique path forward in your life. Change is coming, and staying open to new possibilities attracts an upward trend.

2 Sunday

Developing goals helps improve the priorities in your life. It brings a peachy background that connects with rising possibilities. The wheels are turning in your favor as news arrives, offering a fresh start—opportunities currently circulating in the background move into view. You discover a wellspring of possibilities that lifts the shutters on an enterprising time. Investigating leads draws advancement as you find a side avenue comes calling that brings rising prospects to light.

3 Monday

The Mercury sextile Neptune blends rational thinking with a dreamy aspect. It brings rising creativity and analytical thinking, promoting epiphanies that count. This cosmic alignment helps your dreams become a reality as structured backing behind your vision offers tangible results. Mercury ingress Gemini brings news and information, which adds a refreshing aspect. Communication is light and lively, adding a breath of fresh air to your surroundings.

4 Tuesday

Mercury trine Pluto attracts a questioning aspect that encourages you to dig a little deeper. Delving into what motivates you on a deeper level proves illuminating today. Sun conjunct Venus transit brings peaceful energy, promoting harmony, and focusing on your love relationships and personal bonds. Rekindling vitality brings lighter energy that lets you set sail towards a more social time. News arrives out of the blue, linking you with a productive chapter as you get busy with friends.

5 Wednesday

Several changes ahead help improve your bottom line. You move away from toxic environments, which limits the drama around your social life. You also discover areas that grow your knowledge, opening a prosperous path ripe for progression. Growth and learning are a solid basis for building an approach forward in your life. It brings new responsibilities and a learning curve that deepens your capabilities.

6 Thursday

The New Moon offers a chance to think about the coming month and plan goals that progress life forward. Setting intentions and thinking about your future aspirations help connect with the energy of manifestation to achieve a pleasing result. It is nurturing unique dreams and goals that light up growth pathways in your life. It brings the chance to work with your abilities and deepen your talents in an area that charts a course upward and onward.

7 Friday

Developing your love life helps nurture well-being and happiness as you spend time sharing experiences with a valued companion. You build stable emotional foundations that offer room to progress into a meaningful journey forward for your romantic life. Developing your dreams and being open to sharing with someone who lights up your life enables you to invest your energy wisely as you discover a pathway for your personal life.

8 Saturday

You are doing a fantastic job of improving your life. Indeed, a social aspect ahead brings bright and cheerful energy into your world. Thoughtful discussions with friends harmonize and balance your spirit as it nurtures grounded foundations and draws more stability into your home life. Positive news on the horizon shines a light on expanding your circle of friends. Companionship is key to growing happiness.

9 Sunday

Mars ingress Taurus brings a focus on long-term projects as you work slowly and methodically to achieve your goals. Your willingness to develop a plan and work towards advancement draws a pleasing effect. It offers a proactive time that improves life on many levels. Letting your creativity shine brings new assignments ahead. Rising prospects attract advancement, which nourishes your talents. You weave magic by tapping into options that help you chart a course towards success.

10 Monday

Life is ripe with potential and ready to blossom. It brings choices and decisions that promote rapid expansion as you shift your focus toward developing your career path. Mapping out long-term goals becomes a turning point that enables you to chase your vision and gain traction on improving circumstances. It lets you use your talents to stunning effect as you head towards change. It is a time that offers opportunities for growth and expansion.

11 Tuesday

Mars square Pluto transit brings workplace power struggles and competition. It is a problematic planetary transit that can feel jarring. It can feel disruptive as a sense of chaos can cloud the path ahead. Setting boundaries will ensure you're not fenced in and dealing with challenging power conflicts. If people are selfish or thoughtless, you are wise to distance yourself from the drama. Stepping back from these kinds of situations will help nurture well-being and harmony.

12 Wednesday

Exploring options helps you extend your reach into a new area worth your time. You can reclaim your goals and work towards your vision of a happy and stable career path by being proactive and growing your world outwardly. Inspiring progress leaves you optimistic as you enter a fast-moving environment that offers greater productivity and success. It becomes the gateway from which you deepen your knowledge and advance your skills.

13 Thursday

Life picks up steam, and events ahead set in motion exciting opportunities for your life. Curious changes along bring improvement of circumstances which feels heartening. It lights a social environment that grows your world and tempts you to cross the threshold and enter a brighter chapter in your life. A change of scenery rejuvenates and renews your energy. It promotes lively discussions, which trigger a highly creative atmosphere.

14 Friday

In conjunction with Mercury, the Sun is a favorable aspect that attracts communication. An encouraging, expansive landscape opens up your social life. It brings a cycle of emotional growth that offers an upgrade to your life. It gets more freedom and feels more open as you attract the right synergies into your life. Exploring new possibilities fosters social engagement and provides opportunities to co-create with kindred spirits.

15 Saturday

A social environment ahead sees life on the move as you unpack a journey worth growing. Sharing engaging discussions brings a sunny aspect that builds stable foundations in your life, which nourish grounded energy. Small steps shared with friends add to a meaningful journey of sharing thoughtful ideas and news with kindred spirits. It attracts wellness and harmony, re-fueling your inspiration and drawing laughter and kinship.

16 Sunday

Life brings essential changes which help you move away from adverse environments and embrace a more progressive aspect of your social life. It brings steady progress, which boosts the potential around your life. It promotes a lively time of catching up with friends. It brings a leisurely pace that supports renewal and kinship. Events ahead form a favorable window of opportunity for growing your social life.

17 Monday

Today, the Mercury square Neptune aspect can distort or make mountains of molehills. It adds a dash of illusion into your business dealings that can have your head spinning with tall tales and trying to sort the truth from exaggeration. This area is one of those days that tempt you to expand the barriers and think outside the box to develop workable solutions. Venus slips into Cancer to encourage a focus on emotional well-being and personal bonds.

18 Tuesday

Life brings a significant shift forward as the path ahead clears and opportunities weave into a golden aspect of your life. It offers an enriching time that brings a quickening of pace to your social life. Sharing thoughts with like-minded people nurture stability and happiness in your life. Unexpected serendipity brings companionship and kinship as a meeting of the minds draws close talks. Being with people who resonate on your wavelength nurtures a happy environment.

19 Wednesday

Information arrives, which opens the door to a fresh start. Notable changes attract growth and progression. It encourages you to pour time and energy into developing your social life. As you blaze a trail towards an engaging atmosphere that nurtures a self-expressive and confident vibe, you enjoy a refreshing change of pace that offers expansion. It helps you find your groove as life expands outwardly with friends and companions.

20 Thursday

Today, the Neptune square Sun aspect can water down your ambitions, leaving you feeling foggy and indecisive. If your vision feels clouded, going back over your plans can help make sure they continue to align with your vision for future growth. You discover that expansion arrives in curious ways. Stirring up the winds of change generates new possibilities that carry you forward towards a bright and cheerful landscape.

21 Friday

A sextile between Mercury and Mars sharpens cognitive abilities today. Mental clarity is on the rise, giving you valuable insight into the path ahead. Pursuing personal goals becomes a priority. Enhancements bring advancement into your life. It offers an upgrade that transitions you to an open road of potential. You discover an area that feels right for your soul. A leap of faith lets you make the boldest move towards growing your life in a unique direction.

22 Saturday

The Full Moon brings awareness into your spirit of the areas that seek resolution or adjustment. A time of contemplation draws clarity into the path ahead. It helps you sweep away the outworn areas that hold no future benefits. You have the strength within your spirit to shed outworn regions and improve your circumstances. Seeing the challenges ahead as stepping stones to a brighter future enables you to make the most of growing your life.

23 Sunday

Improvement ahead promotes growth around your home and family life. It brings a productive landscape into view, attracting rising prospects and creating a breezy time shared with friends. A positive influence adds fuel to creativity, and the sharing of ideas charts an auspicious journey towards fresh possibilities. Finding a way to channel your energy into positive outlets brings a pleasing result. It does nurture a happy time in your life.

24 Monday

You can break free of limitations and expand life into new areas. Surprise news arrives with excitement; it highlights new possibilities that spark inspiration. It helps you head towards an environment ripe with blessings. Actively tapping into the potential around your life takes you toward a new assignment that offers growth. It lets you ground your energy in an area that creates a stable foundation. It brings an extended time for creating positive change in your life.

25 Tuesday

You enter a cycle of increasing possibility. You can make the best choices possible as rising confidence helps you follow a journey that brings happiness into your world. It encourages you to move forward in alignment with growing your case as you get busy investigating leads that hold water for your life. Something ahead is ready to kickstart the journey of growth and progress in your life. Nurturing creativity and being open to new possibilities brings a venture that offers rewards.

26 Wednesday

New options help you craft a journey that utilizes your talents to stunning effect. It brings pathways of growth that raise the potential by promoting skills and advancing abilities. It helps extend your reach into a new area worth your time. A spotlight on working with your abilities brings a pleasing result. It enables you to restore stability in what has been an uncertain time. Understanding your inherent strengths and skills helps you head towards advancement.

27 Thursday

An area you discover soon develops into a blossoming path. It brings the chance to work with your abilities and design a journey that promotes your talents to a broader audience. Life settles into an enriching phase that helps you gain traction on advancing your skills. Grounding yourself in the basics lets you get involved with building a sound stage of rising prospects that progresses life forward. You reveal a fresh chapter of exciting options as you refine your abilities.

28 Friday

News arrives that earmarks a unique beginning in your life. It ushers in a busy time that opens a social phase. It brings networking and invitations, which help you plug into a social environment that offers support and connection. Exploring a community setting with friends nurtures well-being and happiness in your life. You soon find your groove in a more social environment that brings opportunities to mingle.

29 Saturday

Venus sextile with Mars draws social engagement into your life. It opens the floodgates to an enriching time that brings invitations to circulate with friends and kindred spirits. Saturn turns retrograde; this aspect focuses on the areas that hold the most significant meaning in your life. Thoughtful discussions enable you to consider new ideas and enjoy additional support consciously. Kindness, caring, and positivity resonate warmly in your life.

30 Sunday

Your life has been one of twists and turns, but you are learning to navigate the hills and valleys of your circumstances with strength and determination. Growth and learning develop your talents and help you create remarkable progress. New options tempt you forward, bringing a unique vantage point where you can see a broader overview of the way ahead. Developing your creativity helps you thrive in a vibrant and dynamic environment.

JULY

Sun	Mon	Tue	Wed	Thu	Fri	Sat
	1	2	3	4	5	6
7	8	9	10	11	12	13
14	15	16	17	18	19	20
21	22	23	24	25	26	27
28	29	30	31			

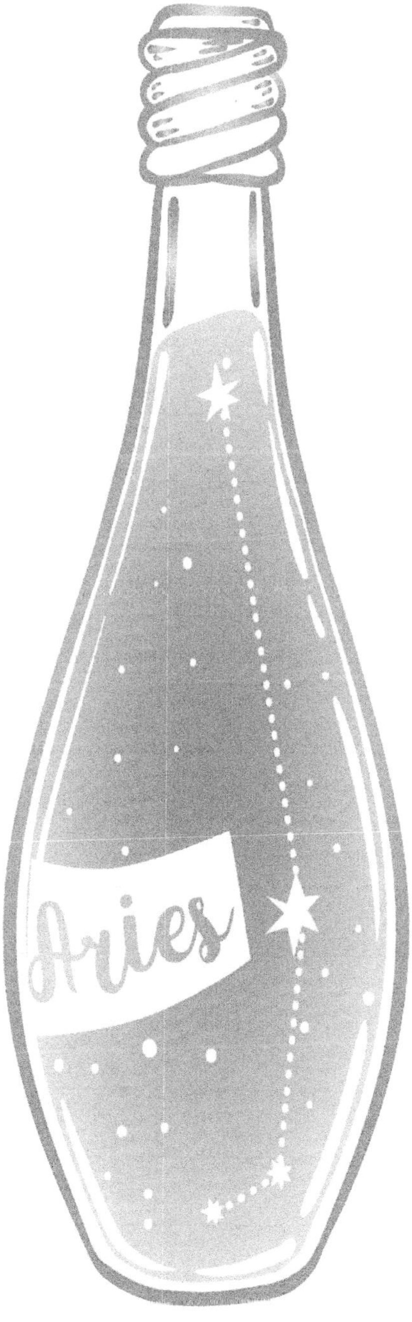
Aries

New Moon

BUCK MOON

JULY

1 Monday

Laying the foundations for improvement holds the key to a new growth cycle. Expanding opportunities offer a trailblazing journey forward toward rising prospects. A positive trend sees life pick up steam as new options emerge in your life. It brings a valuable reward for growing your life outwardly. Amid a time of change, you discover a journey that captures the essence of luck. It cultivates new options that break up stagnant patterns as you develop your skills to the next level.

2 Tuesday

Turning retrograde today, Neptune strips away illusion and any dubious realities which have clouded your vision. At the same time, the Mercury trine Neptune transit stimulates creativity and imagination and fine-tunes your instincts. Mercury ingress Leo adds an expressive vibe that enhances your storytelling and persuasive abilities. A busy time ahead draws new options that light a creative fire in your belly. It has you exploring pathways that foster companionship.

3 Wednesday

Your relationships and social bonds benefit from a steady stream of balanced energy as the Venus trine Saturn contributes loving harmony to your life. Mercury opposed Pluto increases cognitive abilities. It is the perfect transit for researching, developing business ideas, and applying an innovative approach to improving your circumstances. It lights up growth, prosperity, and rising potential. Revision, tweaking, and planning draw a pleasing result.

4 Thursday

A time of transformation places a strong emphasis on improving your life. It repairs broken parts and allows renewal to carry you towards greener pastures. Expansion ahead cultivates greater happiness that nurtures a more social environment. Thoughtful discussions provide clues to future possibilities as you facilitate companionship with someone supportive and engaging. You dip into slipstreams of abundance, which promote positive energy around your life.

5 Friday

Mars sextile sat Saturn adds endurance today, helping you accomplish mundane tasks and keep productive. A New Moon provides the ideal opportunity to map a plan for future growth. New information ahead helps transform your situation towards new possibilities. Developments around your life offer growth and progression. Luck and good fortune are with you and support expansion. The path ahead opens, creating space to develop goals that hold meaning and possibility.

6 Saturday

The changes ahead draw new options into your world. These unique options help you unpack an engaging chapter that offers growth and rising prospects. Happy news ahead keeps your social life humming along. You receive invitations to mingle, which provide a welcome distraction and heightened well-being and happiness. You discover a lot of new energy, which ushers in fresh possibilities. Exploring ways to improve circumstances brings an approach worth your time.

7 Sunday

A change of scene is on the horizon that hits the ticket for rising prospects. It brings a favorable aspect that reboots potential in your world. Your willingness to seek solutions brings new options that let you head towards growth. It enables you to welcome a fresh start that nurtures stability and draws a compelling journey forward in your life. It allows you to touch down a promising path that facilitates developing your social life.

8 Monday

Open-mindedness, curiosity, and a quest for adventure are prominent aspects as a Mercury sextile Jupiter alignment fosters creativity and self-expression. Using your abilities and being resourceful opens pathways of expression and creativity. It rewards with tangible results and options which inspire growth. Tapping into the potential around your life brings a fresh zest that boosts morale. Fanning the flames of inspiration brings creative opportunities that promote your talents.

9 Tuesday

New opportunities are incoming, which inspire you to continue learning and developing your knowledge. Expanding your skills lets you cover all the bases as it shines a flood light on areas suitable for progression. Designing goals opens a journey that elevates your talents and takes you towards options that heighten the potential in your life. Indeed, mapping out new goals brings an exciting destination worth your time.

10 Wednesday

It's a great time to nurture your life and create new foundations that stoke the fires of your imagination. A firm decision ahead brings a journey that offers abundance. Life holds a refreshing change as it provides movement and discovery. It brings a time of reshaping goals as the pace picks up momentum and you head towards a busy chapter. Advancement is in the pipeline, and a new initiative comes calling.

11 Thursday

Venus trine Neptune transit attracts creativity, well-being, and fulfillment. Venus makes a bold statement as she gets comfy in Leo. It is a warmhearted, expressive, generous, and extravagant time. As you expand life outwardly, you weave a web of connectedness in your social life, which brings grounded foundations. You light up a journey of social engagement and expansion that widens your world's borders.

12 Friday

Jealousy may surface as relationships face extra pressure today due to opposition between Pluto and Venus. Focusing on the basics helps ground your energy in daily tasks that foster balance and security. It underscores how important the details of your life can be in restoring harmony. Flexibility and adaptability will help you manage challenging crosscurrents if they surface today. It improves your love life's potential as you become mindful and aware of potential disruptions.

13 Saturday

Being open to connecting with new people cracks the code to a brighter chapter. Change surrounds your situation, and the path ahead suddenly opens when you forge a friendship with someone who inspires you greatly. Combining thoughts and ideas with this person helps you blaze a trail towards developing unique goals. It brings forward momentum that fuels an exciting time in your life.

14 Sunday

Life moves from strength to strength as you develop the path onward. News arrives that brings a bright flavor to your life. It opens the door to a journey that grows your situation in a new direction. It draws a prosperous time to connect with your circle of friends. Circulating in your wider community triggers a cascade of options that let you move forward towards developing companionship in your life. It removes the heaviness and ushers in lighter and more vibrant energy.

15 Monday

Mars conjunct Uranus aspect lets you become more aware of motivations and values and discover the real reasons behind wants and desires. Pursuing your goals helps you push back the barriers as you develop unique dreams which hold meaning in your life. Creativity heightens as you discover pathways that crack the code to improve circumstances. You fuel your dreams and goals with endless possibilities that inspire growth and expansion.

16 Tuesday

You are ready to unpack new options in your life. Exploring a diverse range of pathways enables you to move in a direction that develops your abilities. It brings a change that creates a shift towards a more abundant landscape. You can trust your instincts to guide you as you journey towards advancing your skills to the next level. An original and innovative way forward is a journey that speaks to your spirit.

17 Wednesday

Changes ahead bring new options that offer growth and stability. It helps you gain traction on developing goals as you discover an opportunity previously hidden from sight. Getting involved in cultivating your talents and working with your abilities brings a happy time that offers grounded and secure foundations. It lets you extend your reach to a new area. The more you push back the barriers, the easier it becomes to assert yourself and pursue your dreams.

18 Thursday

Breaking free from limitations and expanding your life brings unique adventures that reveal a journey that blossoms into a meaningful path forward. Crafting your vision for future growth promotes an environment that nurtures your talents. You advance life forward and develop your skills in a new area. You are on a continuous cycle of evolution, growth, and change. Broadening your horizons offers an uplifting trajectory that connects with unique opportunities.

19 Friday

Today speaks of a pivotal time when you can create positive change. Your willingness to unearth new possibilities brings greener pastures. It enables you to open the door to a carefree journey that helps you expand life outwardly. It brings a social environment that offers thoughtful discussions and brings new ideas to the forefront. A sense of connection hits a sweet spot as you share quality time with friends.

20 Saturday

Mars settles into Gemini, which encourages a more diverse outlook. It helps you discover the hidden pathways and journey towards growth over the coming two months. With Mars in your third house, it brings an emphasis on language and communication skills. It opens up avenues of growth and learning which contribute invaluable knowledge. It enables you to refine your communication style to achieve a positive result in your life.

21 Sunday

The Full Moon is a chance for therapeutic healing in your life. If you face a crossroads in your life, going deeper into your goals and aspirations helps provide insight into the path ahead. You are entering a time that rules endings and transitions; it opens into a new chapter that acts as a catalyst for change. Thinking about your life on a deeper level is therapeutic as it facilitates a healing influence. An area you invest time and energy into developing promotes happiness.

22 Monday

A Venus and Jupiter sextile attracts warm and abundant energy into your social life. A dash of luck and good fortune combined with enriching conversations improve social bonds in your life. Original thinking, creative brainstorming, and insightful epiphanies are the order of the day as Mercury squares off against Uranus today. Something new and inspiring flows into your life. The Sun trine Neptune alignment raises the vibration and improves circumstances in your life.

23 Tuesday

The Sun's opposition with Pluto creates a doorway through which pockets of the inner self, spirit, and primal energy can reach the surface of your awareness. It can feel as though you're flying blind but going over the options around your life enables you to sift and sort out the right area for development. Refining and blending your vision for future growth places you in an ideal position to progress life forward towards greener pastures.

24 Wednesday

Good news flows into your life. It helps you lay the groundwork for improving security in your world. Focusing on advancing your vision for future growth lets you make the essential changes that offer rising prospects in your working life. Your willingness to explore leads brings a positive result. It opens the gateway toward growth in your working life. You soon get busy developing skills and learning the path ahead.

25 Thursday

Mercury links up with Gemini, emphasizing connecting with your tribe. You enjoy grounded and stable foundations, which become the basis from which you grow your world. You discover happiness, joy, and fulfillment as you embark on creating positive change in your world. Being open to new people and experiences cracks the code to a brighter chapter as you expand your life outwardly.

26 Friday

The Sun sextile Mars transit brings vital energy and renewed zest for life. The magic courses into your surroundings, bringing options that spark a shift in emotional awareness. It's an environment that encourages creativity to thrive and prosper. Igniting inspiration creates space to grow your talents in a unique direction. You soon reap the rewards of skill development and expansion.

27 Saturday

A dash of adventure adds spice and excitement to your life. It brings an enriching time for following the music in your heart to beat a trail towards your dreams. Focusing on the positive aspects ahead heightens feelings of security and well-being. Improvements abound for your social life as you benefit from events on the horizon. It helps build a bridge towards a brighter chapter. It brings a unique and curious journey that feels right for your life.

28 Sunday

You enter a cycle of increasing abundance that offers a radiant aspect. It carries news and information worth celebrating; it sweeps in the potential that jumpstarts growth. It marks a time of communication that lights the path to a more connected environment. Life fills with magic and excitement as your social life becomes active and dynamic. It triggers opportunities to mingle and connect with friends. Being open to new people and experiences draws a bonus into your social life.

<u>AUGUST</u>

Sun	Mon	Tue	Wed	Thu	Fri	Sat
				1	2	3
4	5	6	7	8	9	10
11	12	13	14	15	16	17
18	19	20	21	22	23	24
25	26	27	28	29	30	31

NEW MOON

STURGEON MOON

29 Monday

Changes ahead bring the opportunity to grow your life in a meaningful area. It offers an enriching chapter that sees you developing your abilities as you chart a course towards growth. Setting unique goals and fine-tuning your vision enables you to cut away from areas that fail to bear fruit. Developing an effective plan helps you make strides in building endeavors that yield enrichment and happiness. It sets the tone for a refreshing time of expansion in your life.

30 Tuesday

Getting involved in developing goals helps manifest a cycle of success. It highlights growing your abilities and extending your reach as you advance towards a lofty goal. Taking inventory of your situation helps pinpoint areas for removal. It brings an optimistic phase that lets you make headway on planning for future growth. It opens the floodgates towards an enterprising avenue that brings an active and vibrant chapter of working towards your goals.

31 Wednesday

A big reveal is coming that lets you set sail on a voyage filled with possibility. A positive trend brings new opportunities to explore. Prioritizing leads and pacing yourself lets you focus on the most significant avenues of growth. It marks a bold beginning in your life as you lay the groundwork for improving your circumstances. An uptick of new options emerges and brings a chapter brimming with potential. It gets the chance to grow your abilities and evolve your talents.

1 Thursday

You soon hone in on new possibilities that inspire growth and progression in your life. Curious changes ahead bring improvement. It rebalances energy as it draws stability into your home life. It creates foundations that offer room to build balance; you enjoy a calming and settled environment that creates space for developing new projects and endeavors. It helps you get inspired by a burgeoning creative enterprise. Acting on instincts draws impressive results.

2 Friday

An increased need for freedom and liberation can destabilize bonds as Venus faces Uranus in a square alignment. If you feel overwhelmed or unsettled, this soon shifts. The tides are turning, and positive influence flows into your world, enabling you to explore new possibilities which light a progressive path forward. Getting involved with side interests recalibrates your emotional slate and brings new development pathways.

3 Saturday

You may find that life is taking you in a new direction, and part of this process is leaving people behind that are not part of your future growth cycle. Cutting away from problematic areas and focusing on the most meaningful path forward will draw a pleasing result that offers a brighter chapter ahead. It brings a time that rejuvenates and reinvents your life on many levels. Mapping out plans helps capture the essence of manifestation to bring new possibilities into your life.

4 Sunday

The New Moon offers a chance to boost your intentions, which can assist you with working with the universe's energy to manifest your goals. Being open to growing new pathways improves the prospects, and results are favorable. Research and learning refine your talents and brings new possibilities into your life. Focusing on vital areas increases potential, enabling you to effectively define your New Moon goals.

5 Monday

Venus ingress Virgo emphasizes practical matters as you build more excellent stability in your home life. Nurturing your home environment creates stable foundations. It brings peace and balance into your world. Releasing external stressors helps nourish your soul and build more security in your life. Rejuvenation is a strong theme that pulls new possibilities into your life and inspires change.

6 Tuesday

The power of intention is essential as planting seeds that bring inspiration and creativity to the forefront of your life. Something you become involved with is a catalyst for change and growth. It brings changes that reveal confidential information. It helps you discover a path forward towards growing your life. It lets you pass the threshold and cross the bridge to a brighter future. It allows you to reinvent yourself and bring light energy into your life.

7 Wednesday

In sextile with Jupiter, the Sun attracts a restless vibe that has you yearning to expand your life outwardly. Expanding your horizons is the perfect way to reinvigorate your surroundings. Far-flung destinations open an ideal avenue to express your restlessness. It does connect you with new adventures that inspire excitement and growth. It brings new people into your circle of friends who share a similar passion for life.

8 Thursday

Mercury conjunct Venus brings the right time to share loving thoughts and receive positive feedback from someone who holds meaning in your life. You let your hair down and communicate openly. It brings a sense of support and connection that draws happiness. Getting involved with friends illustrates a pleasing result. It sparks an enriching journey towards developing companionship and mingling with kindred spirits.

9 Friday

News and invitations appear that brighten your mood. It shines a light on developing friendships and catching up with your broader circle of friends. You benefit greatly from a flurry of activity surrounding your life. Nurturing foundations draws a wellspring of highly compatible options. It brings a purposeful and lively environment that sees things humming along nicely. Fun and friendship light a welcoming path to a more connected chapter.

10 Saturday

A time of self-discovery ahead helps you gain insights into areas best released. It also allows you to discover pathways that offer a ray of sunshine. Intuitive choices bring possibilities into your life. It provides an essential phase of expansion, growth, and opportunity. You are involved in creating a life that smooths rough edges. Taking action is a positive step that builds life from the ground up. You discover the strength, courage, and conviction to overcome challenges.

11 Sunday

As you strive to advance, you reach a crossroads; taking time to think of imaginative solutions lets you chart a course towards growing your life. It helps you sail above life's issues by being open to change and adjusting the path accordingly. A focus on nurturing home and family ties seals the deal on an abundant and nurturing environment. It brings calm and soothing energy into your surroundings. It shores up flagging spirits and opens the path to happiness.

12 Monday

A flurry of activity has you feeling valued and appreciated. Life brings new assignments and projects that are useful in establishing a grounded and balanced environment. New prospects bubble up to keep your creative energy sparking. Significant changes draw good fortune into your world. New possibilities ahead resonate with the essence of wanderlust and adventure. It has you gearing up for a change of pace and seeking to explore a broader world of potential.

13 Tuesday

Finding the right path is essential in cracking the code to achieve your vision. Being adaptable, flexible, and going after creative solutions help unearth the right way ahead for your life. You are setting the bar higher, which forms a vital intention that empowers you to move forward with courage and conviction towards developing your journey through life. An opportunity ahead strengthens your ability to improve your circumstances.

14 Wednesday

Today's Mars conjunct Jupiter transit is ideal for developing goals that require focused energy, initiative, and confidence. Removing the deadwood from the tree enables new blossoms to emerge. It encourages a shift forward that focuses on developing your world with a new approach. Action and thought in motion bring creative energy that leads to a branch of rising prospects. Life picks up momentum and becomes the gateway from which future growth occurs.

15 Thursday

Mercury gets comfy in Leo and brings rising confidence that imbues you with persuasive abilities and an expressive spark that improves communication skills. It draws stabilizing energy that heightens well-being and lights a path towards positive communication and shared experiences. It places you in a prime alignment to enjoy abundance as you solidify foundations and move towards developing your life. It brings opportunities to socialize ahead.

16 Friday

Today's aspect can feel challenging as your mind is on Saturn's to-do list. You may find it difficult to relax and unwind when your thoughts turn to the irons you have burning in the fire. Saturn is a taskmaster; you can harness this energy to achieve a highly productive day. Channeling Saturn's influence enables you to finish the working week efficiently, as forward momentum brings the wind beneath your wings.

17 Saturday

As life heads towards an upward trajectory, you land in an environment ripe with possibilities. You set sail on a timely voyage that expands your life outwardly. Nurturing your life hits a sweet spot that draws abundance into your world. A situation you invest time and energy into blossoms into a path forward. It ushers in a more connected and supportive environment. It sets the stage for an expressive and happy time.

18 Sunday

Original thinking, creative brainstorming, and insightful epiphanies are the order of the day as Mercury squares off against Uranus today. Something new and inspiring flows into your life. Finding the missing element unlocks the gateway toward growth. You reveal a path that makes your goal a priority. Nurturing self-development re-balances emotions and ultimately leads to exploring new interests. It allows you to work with your hands and dabble in a creative area.

19 Monday

Independent thinking and innovative ideas are attributable to the Sun and Mercury conjunct. Today's Venus square Jupiter planetary alignment offers good things for your social life. It is the perfect time to engage with friends; lively discussions nurture creativity. Lastly, the Full Moon brings the chance to clean the slate and heal sensitive areas. Creating space to engage with a healing ritual, such as playing soft music or lighting a candle, helps nurture therapeutic influence.

20 Tuesday

Your ability to manifest and improve outcomes helps nurture a progressive landscape ahead. It brings a pivotal time that enables fundamental changes to draw a stable and grounded environment. As you grow and evolve on this journey, you achieve fantastic results by being willing to work with your abilities and explore new options. You reach a turning point that offers sweeping changes. It brings a refreshing viewpoint that connects you with people and opportunities.

21 Wednesday

You embark on a chapter that focuses on developing key areas of your life. It lets you forge ahead and embrace a lovely time of expanding horizons. Your situation is evolving, bringing new possibilities into your life. Sifting and sorting through options lets you unearth the suitable opportunity to nurture. Setting the bar higher draws the right prospects into your life. Making intelligent choices lets you reach for your dreams. It brings projects and endeavors that inspire you creatively.

22 Thursday

A new influence arrives in your life. It brings opportunities to collaborate and get involved in developing a group opportunity. Giving teamwork a try draws expansion into your life. It gives you a road that nurtures your abilities and grows your talents. It draws supportive and lively ideas that initiate new plans and endeavors. Life improves by degrees; a calming, stabilizing path draws heightened security into your world.

23 Friday

A Venus square Mars aspect can cause challenges as a difference of opinion fosters tension and conflict. Being mindful of staying flexible, understanding, and adaptive will help harmonize bonds and limit the disruption caused by Venus facing Mars at a harsh angle. Being willing to compromise will improve the foundations and limit the disruption in your life. It brings a time of letting go of areas that restrict progress.

24 Saturday

You enter a time of transformation that lifts your spirits higher. It brings a clean sweep of potential that offers growth, advancement, and results. The sun shines brightly over your world as you embark on a journey that sets your heart ablaze with excitement. New opportunities are afoot; life holds change and discovery overhead. It offers a change of scene; a new environment draws more stability into your home life. It brings foundations that are grounded, stable, and happy.

25 Sunday

A new area comes calling; it draws a path that reflects your hopes and dreams. It brings a particular time for expanding horizons and becoming involved in the unique potential that seeks to tempt you forward. It hits the ticket for a journey that draws happiness and harmony. Pushing back the boundaries that surround your life reinvents the potential possible in your world. It brings a green light to connect with creativity and self-development.

26 Monday

The path ahead clears, bringing a succession of events that nurture your abilities. It offers an active cycle of change that attracts the correct type of opportunities into your life. It emphasizes building foundations that draw harmony and stability into your world. News arrives that brings excitement as it lands with a flourish at your door. A dream comes into focus, lighting the path forward. It brings a quickening pace as you extend the barriers of your life.

27 Tuesday

Essential changes offer blessings that feed inspiration and fuel your desire to adapt and grow. You set off on a new adventure that sets an exciting tone for increasing your world. A richly creative process is at the crux of this enterprising time. It draws a gentle element that beautifully accents your current lifestyle. A bright and breezy environment offers a radiant aspect that illuminates new possibilities. It gives your life a reboot and takes you to a happy chapter ahead.

28 Wednesday

Mercury turns direct, bringing a lighter energy flow into your social life. It improves communication and fosters improvement in relationships. The tides turn in your favor as you enter an energizing time that broadens your circle of friends. It brings stable foundations into your life as you deepen a bond with someone who holds similar values and thoughts on life. It brings a sense of fun and excitement into your social life as you mingle and enjoy lively sessions of sharing ideas.

29 Thursday

Venus settles into Libra, raising communication in your life. Personal bonds sweeten, you share ideas, and the opportunity for collaboration heightens. Today's Venus trine with Pluto adds intensity to your love life. This aspect turns up the heat in your personal life. Sexual attraction and passion rise as you get busy developing your personal life. Singles will likely find new romance soon, while couples can embrace a more connected and sizzling love life.

September

Sun	Mon	Tue	Wed	Thu	Fri	Sat
1	2	3	4	5	6	7
8	9	10	11	12	13	14
15	16	17	18	19	20	21
22	23	24	25	26	27	28
29	30					

NEW MOON

Corn/Harvest Moon

30 Friday

Life holds a refreshing change that brings movement and discovery. It involves reshaping goals as news arrives that inspires expansion. It brings a path that offers rejuvenation and happiness. The energy of manifestation surrounds your social life and teams you up with others who grow your world outwardly. Enriching conversations draw a valuable sense of connection with those who support your ideas. Social engagement ahead attracts positive news.

31 Saturday

An emphasis on home and family life secure grounded foundations. It brings a time of relaxation and renewal that lets you focus on the building blocks of your life. It does nurture a positive aspect that heightens well-being. It emphasizes improving your foundations and enhancing the stability possible in your world. It brings invitations flowing into your world that usher in excitement and happiness. It brings opportunities to network with kindred spirits and friends.

1 Sunday

Uranus moving into a retrograde phase boosts idealism; it offers big sky pictures that help motivate change to improve the world around you. This planetary cycle will boost your confidence and foster leadership qualities. It deepens initiative and offers a fresh wind that spurs creativity and an uptick of potential. You amplify the potential by developing solutions that propel you towards greener pastures by using your creative side.

2 Monday

Labor Day. Pluto gets established in Capricorn, the cardinal earth sign. This long transit is character-building. Pluto in Capricorn encourages self-development by magnifying your power and harmonizing your dreams with practical and grounded earth energies. It brings an uptick of potential that helps you move away from a problematic area and nurture a path that feels the right fit for your life. It offers a purposeful time that enables you to make progress on your goals.

3 Tuesday

The New Moon offers a catalyst for change in your life. Planning the path brings stepping stones that lead to a brighter future. The Mars square Neptune aspect brings gossip and scandal to your ears. You hear surprising news that feels disconcerting. Suppose something doesn't ring true to your ears. In that case, you should do your own investigating as this transit could draw misinformation leading to confusion.

4 Wednesday

Mars ingress Cancer brings a chance to diversify your interests and explore new options for your life. You have gifts and talents that are ready to bloom. Reshuffling the decks of potential in your life can rekindle creativity and guide you towards a path that nurtures self-development and personal growth. You exact positive change in your life by being open to growing your skills and extending your reach into exciting areas that hold promise for your life.

5 Thursday

Exciting news arrives that sees the path ahead shining with possibility. It brings a time of rapid change that sparks new goals. Nurturing life brings an enriching journey. It offers a chance to extend your reach into new areas and advance your vision. Lighter energy brings bright and cheerful times, which draws harmonizing foundations. Beautiful symmetry is ahead as you move in alignment with a calling that speaks to your heart.

6 Friday

News flows into your life and stabilizes foundations as it lets you ease troubles and make headway around improving the conditions around your life. Being open to new opportunities and experiences opens the gate to an expressive chapter. It shines a light on growing your world and widening your circle of friends. A situation you invest time and energy into soon blossoms. Seeing your social life expand adds excitement and happiness.

7 Saturday

Mercury and Uranus bring fresh ideas and epiphanies in one of the more positive square alignments. Discovering pathways that take you towards growth offer soul-expanding insights and experiences. It provides a breakthrough that heralds a new chapter in your life. Feeding the fire of inspiration fuels your spirit and helps create a bridge towards a brighter future. It connects you with others who share similar abilities.

8 Sunday

The Sun's opposition to Saturn contributes to limiting beliefs, and this harsher transit can feel challenging. Focusing on the basics helps restore equilibrium. You may be feeling torn about heading in a new direction in your life. Still, this transition can rejuvenate your world from the ground up. Contemplating options brings insight into a remarkable journey forward. Doing some work around releasing limiting beliefs promotes a breakthrough today.

9 Monday

Mercury slips into Virgo to raise analytical powers and provide effective solutions. Your willingness to explore options for your life draws dividends. You hit a home run and begin developing your life outwardly. The conditions are perfect for extending your reach, developing your skills, and refining your talents. Working with your abilities has a powerful effect, providing you with a unique potential landscape. Something on offer soon brightens your day.

10 Tuesday

An opportunity arrives that lights a path forward for your working life. It draws an essential time for advancing goals and developing your skills. It nurtures a strong foundation from which to grow your working goals. Exploring your options unearths a genuine lead that brings new responsibilities and prosperity. Exploring options helps you create a strategy that brings success to your table. Improvement draws a positive influence into your life that heightens security.

11 Wednesday

New energy blazes in and lights a pathway for developing new endeavors. It brings goals that spice up your life with possibility and potential. It draws wellness and balance into your world as you capture the essence of inspiration with plans for future growth. It acts as a catalyst of change for you to begin preparing to embark on a new path forward—it superchargers life with excitement and adventure. Thinking outside the box sees you take a leap of faith into an adventurous chapter.

12 Thursday

A sextile between Mercury and Mars sharpens cognitive abilities today. Mental clarity is on the rise, giving you valuable insight into the path ahead. Today's Sun square Jupiter aspect raises confidence and brings good fortune swirling around your life. Many possibilities support growth and expansion in your life. Being open to growing your situation nurtures your life in many ways. Decisions and choices ahead shape a journey of developing goals and dreams.

13 Friday

A social aspect ahead lifts the lid on new opportunities. It brings a busy time that offers a foundation worth growing. It will seem like you've opened the window and let the fresh air flow into your world. It brings a time that rules expansion, bringing plenty of opportunities to explore. Being open to new people and situations sweetens your journey. It marks a time that is inspired and adventurous. You capture the essence of enthusiasm and merge your dreams with reality.

14 Saturday

Nurturing creativity and experimenting with new pathways bring excitement to the forefront of your life. Have fun exploring refreshing options and see what grows. Your intuition guides you to an opportunity that has room to develop your abilities. It brings a busy and active time of using your talents and getting involved with new endeavors. A highly productive chapter becomes a source of inspiration, leading to a path that progresses skills and elevates prospects.

15 Sunday

The Venus trine Jupiter aspect offers golden threads around your social and love life. It is one of the most anticipated transits which harmonizes interpersonal bonds and offers rising prospects of good luck to your romantic life. It is favorable to those seeking love or wanting a deeper romantic bond. It brings a positive influence that offers your life a brighter, more optimistic vibe. Focusing on improving your circumstances brings a gentle flow of abundance into your world.

16 Monday

As you extend your reach into a prominent area, your career goes from strength to strength. Any issues currently on the periphery of your working life are soon dispersed and put behind you. It brings rapid improvements and an environment that is active and productive. You get established in a dynamic area with room to grow your talents. Life becomes brighter as greener pastures beckon and tempt you onward. It takes in new levels of growth and advancement in your career.

17 Tuesday

Watch for a sign that provides a clue ahead. It brings a lead that sees you working with your talents and refining your skills. It lets you integrate change sustainability to achieve a grounded foundation from which to grow your life outwardly. Things turn a corner, and you soon get busy in a dynamic environment. It brings a new option on offer that advances your life forward. It creates a heightened sense of security that gives you the stability needed to grow your life.

18 Wednesday

The Full Moon draws a healing aspect that helps you detach and move on from outworn areas—setting boundaries and distancing yourself from toxic environments nurtures harmony. Life becomes settled as a healing influence attracts well-being. As Mercury opposes Saturn, it brings heavy vibes into your life. Working with the energies of the Moon helps ease tension and release negativity.

19 Thursday

Today, the Sun trine Uranus aspect adds a dash of spontaneity and excitement into your life. A refreshing change flows into your life, imparts positivity, and draws blessings. It offers opportunities to mingle and network with lively friends and characters. A social aspect sets the tone for an abundant chapter that brings a boost into your life. Opportunities to expand your social circle abound; it introduces you to unique people and creative types.

20 Friday

Notable changes ahead highlight a path of growth and progression. It transitions you to a unique chapter of possibility. You land in a choice environment that offers a social aspect. The future sparkles under this influence, and it brings new people into your life. Heighten opportunities to socialize and nurture interpersonal bonds and friendships. It brings a chapter of relaxed ambiance and thoughtful discussions. It jumpstarts a time of social mixing and improving the foundations.

21 Saturday

Sun opposed Neptune adds a dreamy quality to your day, having you think about prospects. Mercury Square Jupiter adds distraction which brings a lapse of concentration. You may find it challenging to follow conversations and stay on track as your mind tends to wander under this planetary aspect. Dialing back from areas that distract and delay progress enables you to focus on the foundations of your life.

22 Sunday

Sun trine Pluto adds fuel to the creative fire burning within as it increases your desire to gain traction on long-term goals. A positive breakthrough or realization comes calling that lets you spot a journey worth developing. Mapping out goals supports expansion and places you in alignment to grow your world. An area you invest your time into developing draws a pleasing result. New options help cut away from areas best left behind.

23 Monday

You hit the jackpot when a windfall option makes itself known. It lets you negotiate the path ahead and discover golden nuggets of potential. Unearthing new leads gives you a clue of new possibilities that flow into your world to tempt you forward. It has you in sync with expanding your life, which grows your life in a new direction. You carve out time for yourself and embrace rising prosperity. It reveals a positive snapshot of potential that lifts the lid on growing your world.

24 Tuesday

Focusing on improving your career path draws improvement. It advances your job prospects and sees you join a dynamic chapter ahead. Adjusting and refining your goals marks a productive chapter. You streamline your working life and blend your energy into an efficient powerhouse that lets you reach your goals with purpose. It helps create progress; information ahead brings clarity and insight into the blocks that currently hold you back.

25 Wednesday

The Mercury and Neptune opposition helps you communicate your ideas and thoughts today. A dreamy influence have you talking about your vision for the future. It brings a thoughtful effect that encourages you and lets you dare to dream and head toward your goals. Seeing potential projects and future options under the scope of your creativity brings newfound confidence. It allows you to feel confident about developing new plans.

26 Thursday

Mercury trine Pluto offers a spiritual quality that encourages you to head towards discovery as you dig a little deeper into a personal journey. Mercury syncs up with Libra, drawing stable foundations and grounded energy into your situation. It brings news and communication into your life, harmonizing your energy and connecting with others on a similar journey. You enter a phase that sees growth and stability take shape.

27 Friday

Being open to new possibilities helps create a gateway towards growing the potential possible in your world. You ride a wave of hopeful energy as you get back to basics. Your willingness to be open to new people brings golden moments overhead. It puts you in contact with someone who supports and nurtures your life. It draws active and thoughtful discussions and helps you promote a meaningful area. Pouring energy into developing bonds brings a pleasing result.

28 Saturday

Life brings an opportunity to embrace as you move forward and spend time enjoying companionship in a social setting. It draws a path that offers significant growth and expansion. As you chart a course towards developing your life, you enter a bountiful time of increasing potential around your home, social, and family life. It lets you focus on areas that hold the most significant meaning. It offers a unique perspective that rejuvenates your surroundings.

29 Sunday

Your home and family life will be a strong focus as a center of warmth and abundance. It emphasizes creativity; it brings a perfect time to cook up a storm of new ideas and endeavors. Someone in your broader social circle gives you a nudge in the right direction. It brings improvements to your home life, and this offers sweetness and joy. Sharing time with your clan offers enchantment and magic. It brings fun and excitement back into your social life.

October

Sun	Mon	Tue	Wed	Thu	Fri	Sat
		1	2 	3	4	5
6	7	8	9	10 	11	12
13	14	15	16	17 	18	19
20	21	22	23	24 	25	26
27	28	29	30	31		

NEW MOON

HUNTERS MOON

30 Monday

Mars trying Saturn helps you persevere and develop larger goals for your life. Staying flexible and adaptable enables you to pivot towards new possibilities. It brings an extensive chapter on moving into uncharted territory and creates a shift that offers purpose and productivity. The Sun conjunct Mercury aspect favors communication. It brings the sharing of thoughtful dialogues and entertaining discussions.

1Tuesday

A venture you get involved in developing does exceedingly well and opens a productive time in your life. It does bring a learning curve, and developing your skills brings peak performance into the journey ahead. Life sparkles with possibility as you design a course towards a lofty destination. New assignments and options to develop offshoot ventures all add to the excitement around this enterprise.

2 Wednesday

The New Moon brings fresh energy and a sense of wonder last. Being open to developing new ventures brings a sense of purpose and happiness to your life. It is the ideal time to find a new way to move forward constructively in your life. Relishing a new project brings research and planning; it raises the vibration around your life. A buzz of excitement brings new options that hit a sweet note in your life. You head towards a sound chapter of growth and progression.

3 Thursday

There is plenty of potential arriving in your life soon. It helps you gain access to developing an area that offers room to progress and build on. Designing plans brings a buzz of excitement as you feel creatively inspired. It helps you remove limiting beliefs and embark on a journey that offers advancement. It gets an upgrade to your working life that opens a path towards growth.

4 Friday

Today's Venus trine Saturn transit is ideal for developing relationships. Self-expression, warmth, and affection flow freely under this favorable aspect. You attract something you have been seeking, drawing a new cycle into your life that takes your aspirations to the next level. It offers a sparkling path that promotes creative inspiration, freedom, and adventure. It places you in contact with kindred spirits, which lets you become proactively involved in developing your social life.

5 Saturday

Making inroads into developing your situation brings a sense of happiness and abundance into your social life. It helps you create headway on improving bonds which offer room to grow into a meaningful path forward in your life. You glide into a chapter of possibility that acts as a catalyst for change as it kickstarts a breakthrough in your social life. It shines a light on companionship and connection.

6 Sunday

Mercury Square Mars is a harsh alignment that can see disagreements bubble to the surface—thinking before acting can be a saving grace. "Fools dare where angels fear to tread" is an old proverb that speaks volumes about this planetary transit. Pausing to evaluate before acting or speaking on an impulse will serve you well today. Biting your tongue and saving harsh words may be the best action to prevent issues in your social bonds under this short-lived planetary aspect.

7 Monday

When news arrives, the tide turns in your favor, which has you mapping out unique possibilities. It draws information that prepares you to develop a new area that comes calling. Directing your energy towards creating positive change helps you spot a winning trajectory. It brings advancement, and you will soon prosper in a lively environment that develops your skills. The information helps progress the path ahead; it allows you to build more growth around your career goals.

8 Tuesday

Venus trine Mars raises your energy and brings a boost to your life. You make notable tracks on improving your situation as you transition towards new possibilities that encourage growth. Learning new areas lifts the lid on rising prospects that inspire a journey towards greener pastures. It puts you in sync with unique options that offer advancement. Refining your skills facilitates high-level possibilities that provide a rich landscape for your creativity and talents.

9 Wednesday

Jupiter turns retrograde, emphasizing spiritual growth and getting in touch with what truly moves you on a soul level. Self-discovery and personal development become a focus that ends difficulties as you relax in an ambient atmosphere that draws well-being and rejuvenation into your life. Releasing stress nurtures your spirit on so many levels. Something percolating in the background begins to take shape as a potential path forward.

10 Thursday

Information arrives that helps you turn a corner and enter a brighter chapter. As expansion heads your way, it gives you the green light to connect with inspiration. It improves your social life by linking you with others. Mingling with your broader circle of friends sees ideas flowing as possibilities bounce around. It shines a light on stabilizing energies that contribute to rock-solid foundations in your life. An end to difficulties creates a path forward.

11 Friday

Heightened opportunities ahead attract an active phase of growth and development. Sharing thoughts with friends gives you the motivation, courage, and drive to develop new plans for your life. Creativity and concentration are rising, enabling you to organize the path forward for your life. Big sky dreaming sets new possibilities, which position you to grow your world outwardly. It brings opportunities to collaborate and join a group environment.

12 Saturday

Pluto turns direct, bringing an appropriate time to re-evaluate your life. Pluto rules transformation and brings hidden insights to the surface of your awareness when in a moving forward phase. Looking for clues about the path ahead, you soon feel that things are clicking into place as you reveal a new option that feels like the right fit for your life. It brings a unique path forward that lets you touch down on growing your life in a refreshing direction.

13 Sunday

Today's aspect causes a challenging environment as you find your judgment or authority tested. Being challenged and tested feels uncomfortable as you think you are making the right choices and decisions for your life. The Mercury square Pluto transit also attracts interactions with other people who feed the gossip mill and cultivate drama, leading to a toxic environment. Mercury cozies up to Scorpio, bringing a probing and questioning aspect that has you wanting to reveal the truth.

14 Monday

Columbus Day. The Sun forms a trine with Jupiter, which increases good luck and fortune in your life. Being open to new change and possibilities lets you break free from restrictive patterns that prevent life from reaching its highest destination. You move forward towards nurturing a meaningful area that breathes fresh air into your life. Setting intentions provides a mix of manifestation that cracks the code to a brighter chapter.

15 Tuesday

Expect intensity as the Sun square Mars alignment may leave you feeling restless. Venus opposed Uranus's alignment bringing growth to personal relationships. Increasing synergy and chemistry could spark a new romance or flirtation opportunity. It sends positive energy that raises confidence and has you merging thoughts with someone who feels compatible with your life. It spurs imagination and creativity, which offers self-expression and thoughtful discussions.

16 Wednesday

Venus trine Neptune transit attracts creativity, well-being, and fulfillment. It helps you sweep away areas that are no longer relevant and move forward toward new possibilities. News arrives that brings a boost into your world. A situation you nurture takes on a life of its own and brings happiness. It marks a time of renewal that underscores the energy of abundance. It underlines an atmosphere for personal growth and self-development that reflects the person you are becoming.

17 Thursday

The Full Moon helps you turn a corner as you reveal lunar healing, which empowers your life with renewal. It brings a new approach that revitalizes your spirit. Venus settles into Sagittarius, bringing an uplifting, buoyant and optimistic influence. Themes of abundance, security, and happiness enable growing your world in a meaningful direction. Creativity rises as you discover information that lets you transition into a new place of learning.

18 Friday

A friend is looking to reconnect with you to share news and catch up on old times. They have been working on developing career goals and letting the bond with you slide. This person has been thinking and reflecting on the bonds that hold the most significant meaning in their life. It does bring a time of renewing personal bonds and engaging in a lively social aspect that captures the essence of rejuvenation.

19 Saturday

Forgiveness is a valuable tool to rebalance your energy and harmonize personal bonds in your life. If a wound from the past feels raw and sensitive, it's a sign that it needs work to heal and make peace with what has gone before. Releasing outworn energy helps resolve challenging feelings that leave you feeling triggered. It opens a refreshing aspect that nurtures and promotes a clean sweep of potential in your life.

20 Sunday

A welcome piece of news arrives that offers an exciting possibility. As you stand on the precipice of change, you discover new options that encourage expansion in your social life. It lets you turn towards a chapter that highlights abundance, bringing the music flowing sweetly into your world. A happy chapter ahead ushers in new energy. Past struggles fade as you create a fresh start in a meaningful area. Life picks up steam, and plenty of good fortune brings a boost.

21 Monday

You enter a time of expansion that lets you get busy growing your vision. It helps you build a stable phase of growth and prosperity. Cultivating your gifts unearths advancement. It takes your career trajectory higher. It lights a passage towards improving life by being willing to work with your talents and aim high as you head towards a lofty vision. The right conditions ahead hit a sweet note in your career path. A new project overhead drives a purposeful and active journey forward.

22 Tuesday

Mercury trine Saturn adds endurance and gives you extra fuel in your tank to achieve heightened productivity today. The Sun square Pluto aspect draws renewal and rejuvenation. Pluto charts a course towards transformation and offers a highly creative part that lights the way forward towards improving your circumstances. The Sun contributes to golden beams that offer harmony, transcendence, and rising prospects.

23 Wednesday

Changes ahead offer a chance to nurture abilities and advance your skills into an area of potential. Events unfold in due course and offer advancement. It brings an opportunity to reinvent yourself and expand your life outwardly. Utilizing innovative techniques clears a path toward a busy time that provides efficiency and growth. A whirlwind of activity overhead brings new dreams into focus. Pursuing your goals helps you obtain a pleasing result for your working life.

24 Thursday

You turn a corner and soon plot a course towards a new goal. It positions you correctly to improve your life as you direct your energy into achieving a positive result. A cluster of opportunities ahead brings news, projects, and excitement into your life. It carries information on the wind of a new venture that offers room to work with your talents. It brings a chance to escape the humdrum of everyday life. It provides expansion, and it connects you with a more abundant chapter.

25 Friday

Mars sextile Uranus brings unique ideas that help you think outside the box to obtain innovative solutions. Uranus places the focus on rebellion, liberation, and freedom. It adds a dash of spontaneity to your life today. A surge of new possibilities stirs up a sense of excitement. News reaches you that unlocks a gateway towards future growth. Life is active and busy, letting you initiate developing goals.

26 Saturday

News arrives, which offers a chance to follow your passion. It takes your focus off the beaten track when you discover an enticing side journey that gives room to grow your abilities in a new direction. You enter a phase of learning and guidance that shapes the path ahead. It ushers in new energy that has you thinking about the possibilities. It inspires a stage of working towards a fixed goal. Expanding your life leads to a memorable phase that creates positive change.

27 Sunday

Surprise news brings tremendous changes to your home life. You move forward with a clear head that enables progress to occur. Taking care of business, you soon get cracking on developing your vision. Honing in on your true purpose marks a necessary time of transition that sees elevated potential flowing into your world. Using the energy of manifestation lets you fast-track a cycle of growth. Ramping up the success rate brings momentum that offers progress.

28 Monday

Under the influence of a Mars and Neptune trine, creativity soars, and epiphanies and lightbulb moments are the order of the day. Exploring thoughts and ideas takes your imagination to impressive heights. It teams you up with a joint project that offers collaboration, networking, and communication. Weeding out distractions lets you focus on nurturing the potential possible. Setting intentions and mapping out plans for future development is constructive.

29 Tuesday

An opportunity comes knocking; it creates space to chase a dream. As you take those tentative steps to improve your situation, information arrives; it lets you hit your stride and progress forward. You gather the assistance of someone effective in evaluating ideas and offering advice. It brings a time of brainstorming sessions that see innovative solutions rising. It brings a burst of inspiration to your creative process. It delivers results and offers room to advance your situation.

30 Wednesday

The Mercury opposed Uranus transit bringing a chaotic and hectic pace. The busier pace may leave you feeling tense, anxious, and scattered. Uranus adds a dash of the unexpected, leaving you scrambling to deal with surprise news. Information emerges from the blue, leaving you wondering what will happen next. Focusing on the basics today improves balance and lets you integrate change sustainably in a grounded manner that grows your life.

31 Thursday

A positive influence brings greater possibility into your world. It brings energy and excitement into your social life. Entertaining and mingling with friends begin an extensive phase of drawing happiness and harmony into your life. Sudden news arrives that brings an invitation too good to pass up. It opens the door to opportunity and expansion. A spontaneous sense of wanderlust connects you with others who resonate with the same wavelength.

NOVEMBER

Sun	Mon	Tue	Wed	Thu	Fri	Sat
					1 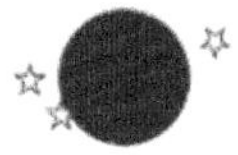	2
3	4	5	6	7	8	9 
10	11	12	13	14	15 	16
17	18	19	20	21	22	23 
24	25	26	27	28	29	30

Aries

NEW MOON

BEAVER MOON

NOVEMBER

1 Friday

Creativity, imagination and innovation blaze a wildfire of inspiration as Mercury and Neptune form a trine today. Increased sensitivity to this vibrational energy attracts a boost into your world that bolsters vitality. It offers a dramatic shift that helps you quickly learn or develop a new area. Making intelligent choices leads to a breakthrough. It does encourage advancement as you head towards growth. You can harness the New Moon's energy today to start something new in your life.

2 Saturday

A Mercury trine Mars aspect attracts a restless vibe. This cosmic alignment leaves you feeling spontaneous and ready for new adventures today. It links you to a path that brings gifts and luck. It captures the essence of wanderlust and offers an exciting journey forward. A creative aspect helps bring artistic expression out in the open. An expressive and trailblazing time following your heart begins a positive trend that expands your life.

3 Sunday

Mars opposing Pluto brings a drive to succeed and gain traction on growing your long-term goals. Venus opposes Jupiter and brings good fortune into your romantic life. It adds an indulgent vibration and has you wanting to explore hedonism, romance, and magic. You soon break fresh ground when news arrives, with an inspiring and exciting chapter ahead. It places a spotlight on personal growth and love connections.

4 Monday

Mars ingress Leo raises confidence and helps you go boldly into uncharted territory to achieve growth in your life. Additionally, today's Sun trine Saturn offers constructive dialogues and thoughtful ideas that enhance your creativity and stimulate new pathways of possibility in your life. It does open a path towards rising prospects, which helps you achieve a beneficial result for your career path. Lightness and momentum bring a productive and busy working environment.

5 Tuesday

You see changes around your life that offer progression and advancement. All in all, it improves your life's stability by giving you more options to explore. It places you in the box seat to expand life outwardly and extend your reach into new areas. New opportunities arrive that lead to a stable phase of growth. It brings a chance to improve circumstances as it shines a brilliant path towards developing your goals. It helps remove blocks and progress life in an enterprising area.

6 Wednesday

Life is ripe with potential and ready to blossom. It brings fresh ideas that let you see the path ahead clearly. You reveal a landscape of exciting options that draw a purposeful and innovative journey towards an active and productive environment. It lets you make progress around some of your larger goals. Chasing your dreams is a vital priority and takes you towards embracing a path of growth. Issues that limit progress soon fade away as the sunshine blooms in your world.

7 Thursday

Changes ahead bring inspiration flowing into your life. A focus on building your dreams draws a pleasing result. Immersing yourself in an exciting area gives purpose and substance to your world. It helps set up a long-term structure around your home life. It brings goals to work towards, and many possibilities flow into your world; each represents something new on offer. It brings a time of personal growth that enriches your life. You breeze through an ample time of opportunity.

8 Friday

Things begin to shift forward when an opportunity in your local community crops up. It reveals new information that helps transform your situation towards brighter pathways of growth and prosperity. Luck and good fortune are with you on this journey towards expansion. News arrives that brings a path worth growing. A social vibe ahead brings many possibilities flowing into your life. You step out on a new adventure and harness a sense of excitement.

9 Saturday

An enterprising chapter ahead brings choices that offer remarkable change. Immersing yourself in opening your world to new people and experiences draws a pleasing result for your life. It sparks a refreshing shift that releases troublesome energy and brings a stable calming influence into your life. The results are an abundant chapter that lets you place a unique stamp on improving your life. Becoming proactive in developing goals helps you manifest a cycle of success.

10 Sunday

As you head down the river of life, there will always be a few riverbed rocks that create turbulence. Learning how to navigate downstream towards calmer waters helps grow your experience. It brings skills and abilities that enable you to balance life's ups and downs without becoming adrift. Taking time to process and integrate changes in your life draws a stable foundation. Your willingness to expand horizons and set sail on new adventures brings a pleasing result.

11 Monday

Venus ingress Capricorn draws grounded energy that has you feeling capable of developing stable foundations in your life. Channeling energy into family bonds nurtures more excellent stability in your home life. It brings positive energy, happiness, and harmony to your family situation. You reveal answers that bring improvement to your home life. It highlights a warm and inviting time shared with people who hold the most significant meaning in your life.

12 Tuesday

A block may prevent you from achieving peak performance today as Mercury square Saturn creates challenges around communication and sharing free-flowing ideas. This transition can feel jarring, and creating space to release outworn areas helps nurture a time of renewal and rejuvenation. It brings the chance to cut away from areas that are no longer part of the journey. Clearing the blocks around your life helps you establish new foundations.

13 Wednesday

As you gain traction on advancing life forward, you discover an enterprising journey that offers progress. Serendipity lights the way ahead, bringing new possibilities into your life. Change is coming; staying open to growing your life attracts an upward trend as you discover an avenue to revolutionize the path ahead. Channeling your energy into nurturing your dreams brings a comprehensive approach that provides a pleasing result.

14 Thursday

Changes ahead get the ball rolling on a social chapter that offers improvement. It creates space to nurture well-being. You draw rejuvenation and balance into your surroundings. It brings the sharing of thoughts and ideas with others that attracts abundance, which supports and grows your life in a unique direction. Good news arrives that illuminates a path forward. It teams you up with investing in your talents and triggers a pleasing outcome.

15 Friday

Saturn turns direct, lifting the shutters on an enterprising chapter that sees forward propulsion moving you towards beneficial outcomes for your life. The Full Moon draws a therapeutic influence that reboots your energy and wipes sensitive areas from your spirit. Scheduling outworn areas for deletion brings a focus on improving circumstances that boost your spiritual, mental, and psychological well-being.

16 Saturday

Exploring options opens a path that offers room to progress life forward. It puts you in contact with others who bring a valuable sense of support and connection into your world. It rules a time of increasing expansion and harmony. It creates foundations that offer room to grow your circle of friends. It sets the stage for a beautiful journey towards nurturing your life. It brings a carefree and happy time that lets you relax and mingle with your broader circle of friends.

17 Sunday

The Sun opposed Uranus transit attracts a restless vibe that gives you the green light to try something new and different. It drives a liberating chapter that offers spontaneity as you get busy expressing your unique individual melody and personality. A sense of wanderlust guides your vision as you chart a course towards exploring new leads. It lets you nurture a wellspring of abundance as you shape new goals and connect with a broader world of possibility.

18 Monday

Today, Mercury opposed Jupiter draws a favorable aspect that nurtures good fortune in your social life. A surge of well-being and potential hits the sweet note in your social life. It marks a festive time that encourages interpersonal bonds. New options ahead leave you feeling inspired and optimistic about the future. You reach a turning point and grow a journey that offers rising prospects for your life. It helps push barriers back, marking a refreshing time that rules expansion.

19 Tuesday

New possibilities ahead light a fire of potential in your belly soon. It sparks a journey that offers growth and progress. It lets you diverge from everyday routines and diligently use skills and abilities. Being productive garners recognition; it provides a chance to give back to others. It has you feeling optimistic about the prospects ahead. As you direct your energy towards expanding your life, you discover opportunities that help you thrive and prosper.

20 Wednesday

New possibilities ahead and ramp up the potential in your life. It offers a chance to head towards growth and gain traction on progressing your dreams. Taking time to plan and plot a course forward ensures a stable shift occurs as you embark on developing the potential possible in your world. It lifts the lid on an enterprising chapter that offers an efficient and productive phase of growing a path towards rising prospects.

21 Thursday

Today's Sun sextile Pluto transit drives ambitions and sees you heading into your work with an increased drive to succeed and conquer your goals. Valuable rewards are on offer if you stay focused and grow your world. Information arrives that helps you build something tangible and concrete. It increases your skills and deepens your understanding of the path ahead. It leads to a busy time of gaining skills that offer advancement.

22 Friday

Today, Venus sextile Saturn promotes cooperation and offers the chance to join a joint project. News arrives that highlights a path of creativity, self-expression, and possibility. You discover a richly abundant journey that lights a new way forward in your life. It brings a time of collaboration and progress that draws rising prospects into your social life. New energy is brewing, and opportunities to mingle ahead draw a vibrant atmosphere of social engagement.

23 Saturday

Prepare to make room for new friends and companions. An invitation ahead lightens the atmosphere in your social life. It brings exchanges with friends and sees more liveliness emerging in your life. Life gets a refreshing change of pace. It brings a joyful time of nurturing friendships that casts a light on the exciting potential that shifts your focus forward. It triggers an active phase of movement and discovery that entices you to grab the reins as you journey onward.

24 Sunday

Adventure comes calling and lets you chart a course towards a boatload of potential. Friends and family connect, and an option to use technology connects you with someone who has lately been out of the loop. A pioneering attitude pushes boundaries back and draws higher opportunities to deepen a bond. It brings conversations that are tailor-made for renewing a situation. It sparks a friendly time of catching up.

25 Monday

A shift ahead transitions you towards a positive chapter that brings sunny skies overhead. It opens the doors to a busy time that sees you sharing with friends and family. It brings a positive social aspect that draws well-being and harmony. It places you in a solid position to get involved with a more social path. It strongly correlates to improved security and stability on the home front. A social chapter ahead washes away the stress and outworn energy.

26 Tuesday

Mercury turns retrograde, which creates a challenging environment for growing personal bonds. Miscommunication is more prevalent during this planetary cycle, leading to communication blocks and misunderstandings in your life. Setting boundaries with people who cause issues hold you in good stead as it develops your world in the right direction. You have the strength and fortitude to overcome barriers during the retrograde phase and move toward expansion.

27 Wednesday

Sun trine Mars raises creativity and highlights positive energy around your thought processes. Communication arrives to tempt you out in the broader community. It aligns you with the direction of growing your social life. It offers a time of insightful dialogues that illustrates increasing stability and balance in your world. An enriching time shared with others provides a fresh start on many levels. It reawakens you to a broader world of potential.

28 Thursday

Thanksgiving is a time that focuses on family. A social aspect brings harmony overhead. It does offer an influx of possibilities that rules expanding your social life. Improvement on home territory becomes the main focus; it draws inviting potential that strikes a chord as it hits a positive note for your life. You are mindful of the blessings in your life, bringing gratitude to the surface today.

DECEMBER

Sun	Mon	Tue	Wed	Thu	Fri	Sat
1	2	3	4	5	6	7
8	9	10	11	12	13	14
15	16	17	18	19	20	21
22	23	24	25	26	27	28
29	30	31				

New Moon

Cold Moon

29 Friday

Life heads towards an upward trend that enables you to share with your broader circle of friends. Networking and mingling promote growth in your love life. It brings a heightened opportunity to share open communication and enjoy a relaxing and ambient environment. It offers bonding share sessions that hearten and enrich your life. It all translates to a good time for growing your love life in the right direction.

30 Saturday

Your willingness to open your life outwardly draws unique options. It offers more time shared with friends as a social aspect brings exciting opportunities to light. Communicating with your network of companions re-fuels inspiration and inspires growth in your life. It promotes a happy, optimistic chapter that buoys your spirit and uplifts your life with refreshing potential. Invitations, and news, are prevalent.

1 Sunday

The December New Moon brings an empowering aspect as new opportunities arise, boosting your support networks. Information and developments help nurture a unique perspective and outlook on life. It draws a busy, active time that creates steady improvement with a grounded foundation. Thoughtful dialogues bring a boost to your world. It is a time that inspires your life on many levels as it draws well-being and renewal to your door.

2 Monday

A Venus trine Uranus aspect adds a dash of spontaneity and fun to your life. A landmark time brings new possibilities into your social life. It offers a chance to catch up with your broader circle of friends. Connecting with your tribe draws an active chapter that captures the essence of happiness. It provides a bright outlook as new energy cultivates friendships and draws vitality into your spirit. It brings a busy time that marks a journey where significant change is possible in your life.

3 Tuesday

Things are on the move in your life when good news lands with a flurry of excitement. It draws a sweet chapter filled with lively conversations as an invitation to mingle opens your life up to a new environment. Developing your social life is instrumental in bringing goodness to the surface of your world. It opens a journey that draws connection and companionship.

4 Wednesday

Mercury opposed to Jupiter, brings positive communication and news. Saturn is the ruler of honoring traditions. Today's square with the Sun illuminates a happy time shared with loved ones, perfect with Saturn, who delights in celebrating established bonds. Venus sextile with Neptune sends loving beams into your home and family life, harmonizing bonds and drawing the essence of rejuvenation and renewal to your door. She builds grounded and stable energy around your life.

5 Thursday

As your life turns full circle, you discover a chance to turn back the clock and reconnect with someone who inspired your life back in the day. You get a glimpse of a compelling journey that offers a social aspect that feels good for your soul. It places a spotlight on developing a bond worth your time. Growing your social life brings constructive dialogues and opportunities to engage with people who enrich your life.

6 Friday

Mars retrograde offers a chance to remove hidden blocks that prevent progress from occurring in your life. It is the appropriate time to confront aspects you usually repress. Now is the time to dig deep and look at any unresolved conflicts limiting your true potential. You accomplish a great deal by focusing on the building blocks of your life. Consistency, determination, and effort build a bridge towards a brighter future.

7 Saturday

Venus ingress Aquarius brings a desire to connect with people who resonate on your wavelength. Venus, the ruler of love, offers an abundant landscape when conjunct with Pluto. The energy of transformation surrounds your life, enabling you to advance your romantic life. Manifesting your happiness is on the agenda as you deepen your romance aspirations and grow the potential possible in your love life. You begin to see what is possible when you expand the borders of life.

8 Sunday

Venus opposed Mars, increasing drive, chemistry, and sexual attraction. Life brims with possibility. You are ready for a new chapter that enlivens your social life. It lets you swim upstream and discover smoother waters that offer stability and attract abundance into your life. The magic of possibility fuels inspiration, and creativity rise, bringing new options to light. A path opens that represents the beginning of a journey that grows your experience.

DECEMBER

9 Monday

A stroke of luck and a serendipitous snippet of news lets you put the puzzle pieces into place. It helps you map out a plan for future growth and mark out the stepping stones necessary to advance life. As the conditions for growth ripen, you begin to receive more security and stability. It is a good indicator that things are heading in the right direction for your life. Working towards your dreams brings progress that feels like validation. It does have you feeling a sense of accomplishment.

10 Tuesday

A social chance to mingle with friends hits the right music for your world. As communication arrives out of the blue, it lets you bridge the gap with people you haven't seen for a while. It rebalances your spirit after a busy time and directs your attention towards nurturing interpersonal bonds in your life. It brings a journey that offers unique experiences, companionship, and new potential. It brings a time of chasing dreams and engaging in lively discussions.

11 Wednesday

Life turns full circle and reconnects you to the past. It brings news and information into your life, drawing the winds of change into your world. A friend from a previous chapter bridges the gap to catch up with you. This person has fond memories they hold dear to their heart. It emphasizes nurturing a personal bond as you set sail on a timely voyage of developing a unique path forward.

12 Thursday

Your dear and valued friend connects to catch up with you. This person has been going through some significant life changes and seeks your support as they share news of a new venture in their world. It lets you touch on an enterprising chapter that nurtures companionship, harmony, and happiness. Blending ideas and designing a journey ahead with this person draws an exciting time that captures the essence of creativity.

13 Friday

Today's Mercury sextile Venus adds a positive influence that harmonizes and nurtures well-being in your world. Less stress and more enjoyment grow solid foundations. Personal relationships benefit from open communication leading to fulfillment. It provides an impressive pathway that creates a platform from which to expand your world. It ushers in an expressive social aspect that cultivates lively discussions, engagement, and sharing with friends and companions.

14 Saturday

An undercurrent of rising possibility surrounds your romantic life as transformation sweeps in to encourage connection development. It brings lighter energy that lays the groundwork for a stable situation to flourish in your love life. Sharing thoughtful dialogues with another opens an engaging and refreshing journey. Nurturing your love life brings a winning chapter into view as you chart a course towards improving circumstances.

15 Sunday

A glorious Full Moon helps you turn a corner. It signals a chance to heal the past and go beyond what you thought was possible. It can bring out strong emotions, and finding therapeutic ways to channel these sensitive feelings positively draws healing. Mercury turns direct, which releases negativity around personal and social bonds. Any crosswires during the retrograde phase will soon lift as lighter energy attracts a positive influence in your life.

16 Monday

An opportunity ahead helps you redesign your life from the ground up. It connects you with kindred spirits who support growth. You attract positive energy and possibilities that help you advance life forward. Lively discussions with creative companions help blend trailblazing ideas into a path of potential. It highlights a social aspect that brings people together in a group environment. It offers a journey with room to grow your talents and discover your purpose.

17 Tuesday

Positive change ahead brings goodness to the top of your world. It unearths new possibilities for your social life. It brings opportunities to develop a more prosperous home and family life. The seeds you plant mark a new beginning. It triggers an original path that heightens creativity and lets you plan future dreams and goals. It helps you see your life from a unique perspective that is heartening. It offers in-depth conversations that draw well-being into your world.

18 Wednesday

A social aspect ahead lifts the lid on new opportunities. It brings a busy time that offers a foundation worth growing. It will seem like you've opened the window and let the fresh air flow into your world. It brings a time that rules expansion, bringing plenty of opportunities to explore. Being open to new people and situations sweetens your journey. You capture the essence of enthusiasm and merge your dreams with reality.

19 Thursday

A positive trend opens the door to a fresh start. It marks a bold new beginning. It brings a shift towards expansion that extends the borders of your life. Events on the horizon offer a chance to mingle and network. A social aspect gets a sweet surprise that shines the spotlight on nurturing abundance in your world. Thoughtful conversations bring an opportunity to join forces with someone who offers the gift of companionship to your life.

20 Friday

You sail through a breezy time of heightened opportunities for socializing. It brings rising possibilities that spark a journey of abundance and joy. You soon begin to see steady improvement flowing into your romantic life. It brings an engaging time of expansive horizons that lets you explore a social environment with a twist of romance and adventure. This social landscape draws entertaining dialogues and meaningful moments.

21 Saturday

Good news arrives for you and brings an emphasis on fun and friendship. Your social life becomes a focal point as surprises come to keep you feeling inspired by life. You build robust bonds that have room to deepen over time. A change of scenery feels therapeutic and brings lighter energy into your world—communication hums along as you share thoughts with others who offer support and kindness.

22 Sunday

Memories of the past crop up in your life to remind you of your journey. Keeping treasured moments close to your heart draws well-being and happiness. Nurturing balanced foundations around your life creates a solid basis for launching new endeavors. You can trust your instincts to guide you as you open your life to a unique flavor that offers rising prospects. Information ahead cracks the code to a bright chapter.

23 Monday

A social aspect lightens the atmosphere in your life. It brings a refreshing change of pace. It washes away outworn energy and creates space to nurture interpersonal ties. Spending time with valued friends and companions draws rejuvenation. It brings a broader landscape of potential that casts a rosy glow over your life. It brings a time of thoughtful discussions and a journey that resonates with future goals. It puts the icing on the cake when you discover rising potential ahead.

24 Tuesday

The Jupiter square Saturn aspect signifies overspending could bring a crimp to your finances. If you feel a little blue about financial prospects, creating a budget and planning to repay the credit cards in time will help you balance your money woes. You soon absorb this information and get busy planning future goals. Mapping out a strategy is helpful as it gives you the building blocks of your future vision. An organized approach provides a winning trajectory.

25 Wednesday

A positive influence strengthens foundations. It creates space to nurture a time of fun, leisure, creativity, and social engagement. A strong emphasis on home and family life brings forward-facing momentum that offers lighter energy. It draws balance and harmony into your life, and the positive aspects ahead offer noticeable growth. It brings lively exchanges and opportunities to mingle. It emphasizes improving home and family life.

26 Thursday

Today, Mercury is the show's star and draws a favorable aspect that nurtures good fortune in your social life. It brings a chance to share with friends and loved ones. Relaxing and unwinding enable you to restore frazzled nerves and build robust foundations. You enter a time of inspiration, manifestation, and engagement with friends. A more social aspect brings a breath of fresh air into your surroundings.

27 Friday

Mercury square Saturn challenges social talks. Tensions could flare up and lead to disruptions. Miscommunication is more likely when you are not on the same page as the person you talk to about your thoughts and ideas. Focusing on open and transparent communication can help you be on the same wavelength during this challenging aspect. Being mindful of moving with grace and harmony draws a pleasing result today.

28 Saturday

You turn the corner and head towards rising prospects that nurture a fantastic result for your love life—romance and magic course through a time of developing companionship and nurturing a bond of the heart. You discover the great potential that elevates the energy around your romantic life. It enables you to open a fresh chapter that nurtures harmony, connection, and well-being. It brings a beautiful result into your world.

29 Sunday

Something currently percolating in the background of life will make a vivid appearance soon. It offers a splash of color and a dynamic vibe that opens the gate toward growth and change. It brings a passage forward that marks the beginning of a new journey. As you soon discover a lead worthy of development, life moves from strength to strength. Navigating an ever-changing environment brings adaptability that lays the groundwork for a stable basis to grow your world.

30 Monday

You finish the year on a high note as news arrives, opening the floodgate to developing your love life. Surging possibilities fuel inspiration which connects you with a wellspring of happiness. A landscape of entertaining discussions, weave magic around your romantic aspirations. Lively and engaging sharing creates space to nurture companionship in your life. It brings romance and light to your door.

31 Tuesday

Mingling with your broader circle of friends opens life up to a new flavor. It promotes a carefree and engaging time that sets the stage to establish a grounded foundation around your life. Linking up with kindred spirits brings an expressive time that facilitates lively discussions as you touch down on an abundant landscape. Change swirls around your life as you head towards expansion.

1 Wednesday

Developing social ties and expanding horizons draw benefits. It brings people into your life that inspire your mood as they cultivate a meaningful bond with you. It opens a journey of change, adventure, and excitement. You head towards a happier and more expressive time that enables you to optimize your life. Sharing with kindred spirits brings fresh inspiration into your world.

2 Thursday

Good fortune enters your life as you touch on a favorable chapter imbued with possibility. Expect improvement in social areas as incoming news breathes fresh air into your social life. It opens a journey of new ideas and opportunities that capture the essence of excitement as you get ready for a fresh start. It ushers in a positive aspect that brings blessings into your world. An invitation to mingle brings the magic coursing into your life.

Astrology, Tarot & Horoscope Books.

Mystic Cat

Made in the USA
Monee, IL
04 January 2024

50905262R10096